WHAT IF YOU WERE GOD?

21-DAY WORK AND PRAYER BOOK TO FIND YOUR INNER SUBSTANCE

by Andrea Elizabeth

Copyright 2020 Andrea Elizabeth

This book is copyright under the Berne Convention. All rights reserved.

No Reproduction without permission.
Printed in the United States of America

ISBN: 978-1-7346885-0-4

CATALOGING INFORMATION:

Elizabeth, Andrea

What if You Were God?

21-Day Work and Prayer Book to Find Your Inner Substance

Filing categories:

OCC032000 BODY, MIND & SPIRIT/Angels & Spirit Guides

OCC011010 BODY, MIND & SPIRIT/Healing/Energy (Qigong, Reiki, Polarity)

OCC011020 BODY, MIND & SPIRIT/Healing/Prayer & Spiritual

BIO018000 BIOGRAPHY & AUTOBIOGRAPHY/Religious

SEL006000 SELF-HELP/Substance Abuse & Addictions/Alcohol

BIB020050 BIBLES/The Message/Study

....

Andrea's websites:
www.spiritualenergyhealingguide.com
https://www.beurownreligion.com/

Facebook: https://www.facebook.com/andreaelizabeth2020/

YouTube: https://www.youtube.com/channel/UCCX0V_sGJTh9wDZlA0WLPyA/featured?view_as=public

Patreon: https://www.patreon.com/AndreaElizabeth

Table of Contents

Author's Note v
Prologue – About Andrea Elizabeth vi
Chapter 1 – Andrea Elizabeth: My Story 1
Chapter 2 – The Untrusting Soul Space.................... 8
Chapter 3 – Day 1: Peeking Inside Our Truth 15
Chapter 4 – Day 2: Willingness to Change 22
Chapter 5 – Day 3: Self-Deception to Truth
  With the Australian Aboriginals............................ 27
Chapter 6 – Day 4: Accomplishments..................... 31
Chapter 7 – Day 5: Holiness 35
Chapter 8 – Day 6: The Holy Sacraments
  With Master Jesus 41
Chapter 9 – Day 7: Creating Newness
  With Master Jesus 43
Chapter 10 – Day 8: The Universal Mind
  With Pythagoras 48
Chapter 11 – Day 9: Finding your Magnificence
  With Pythagoras 52
Chapter 12 – Day 10: Creating Vows of My Soul
  With Moses 55
Chapter 13 – Day 11: Finding Grace Within With
  Our Blessed Mother.. 59
Chapter 14 – Day 12: The Unseen Forces Within
  With Our Blessed Mother and the
  Heavenly Angels.. 70

Continued

Chapter 15 – Day 13: Commingling Assets
With Master Jesus 75
Chapter 16 – Day 14: Relevant to God With
Einstein and Sir Isaac Newton 80
Chapter 17 – Day 15: The Journey of Self-
Enlightenment 94
Chapter 18 – Day 16: The Enrichment of Your Soul
With Master Buddha, our Blessed Mother, and
Divine Master Kwan Yin 102
Chapter 19 – Day 17: The Road to Enlightenment
Through Nirvana With Master Jesus
and Master Buddha 106
Chapter 20 – Day 18: The Road to Enlightenment
Through Nirvana With Archangel Michael,
and Master Lento 110
Chapter 21 – Day 19 138
Chapter 22 – Day 20: Humility With
Master Jesus 153
Chapter 23 – Day 21 162
Conclusion 177

Chapter 15 – Day 13: Commingling Assets
With Master Jesus 75
Chapter 16 – Day 14: Relevant to God With
Einstein and Sir Isaac Newton 80
Chapter 17 – Day 15: The Journey of Self-
Enlightenment 94
Chapter 18 – Day 16: The Enrichment of Your Soul
With Master Buddha, our Blessed Mother, and
Divine Master Kwan Yin 102
Chapter 19 – Day 17: The Road to Enlightenment
Through Nirvana With Master Jesus
and Master Buddha 106
Chapter 20 – Day 18: The Road to Enlightenment
Through Nirvana With Archangel Michael,
and Master Lento 110
Chapter 21 – Day 19 138
Chapter 22 – Day 20: Humility With
Master Jesus 153
Chapter 23 – Day 21 162
Conclusion 177

Table of Contents

Author's Note v
Prologue – About Andrea Elizabeth vi
Chapter 1 – Andrea Elizabeth: My Story 1
Chapter 2 – The Untrusting Soul Space.................... 8
Chapter 3 – Day 1: Peeking Inside Our Truth 15
Chapter 4 – Day 2: Willingness to Change 22
Chapter 5 – Day 3: Self-Deception to Truth
   With the Australian Aboriginals........................... 27
Chapter 6 – Day 4: Accomplishments..................... 31
Chapter 7 – Day 5: Holiness 35
Chapter 8 – Day 6: The Holy Sacraments
   With Master Jesus.. 41
Chapter 9 – Day 7: Creating Newness
   With Master Jesus.. 43
Chapter 10 – Day 8: The Universal Mind
   With Pythagoras 48
Chapter 11 – Day 9: Finding your Magnificence
   With Pythagoras 52
Chapter 12 – Day 10: Creating Vows of My Soul
   With Moses 55
Chapter 13 – Day 11: Finding Grace Within With
   Our Blessed Mother... 59
Chapter 14 – Day 12: The Unseen Forces Within
   With Our Blessed Mother and the
   Heavenly Angels... 70

Continued

Author's Note

As I am revising this book, I find it necessary to elaborate more about God. The idea for this book came about with the intention of helping one realize that we are all God inside. Not God as a man-made name given to a spiritual substance, not God as a person or a man, and not God as a deity. I bring to you the best definition I have found, so far, and it came from the Messages from Matthew blog posts written by a mother whose son died at a young age, but comes back and gives her information from the other side. He said that "We are the Essence of Unconditional Love Expressed as Light." And this hit the perfect chord in me, as that is exactly the purpose of this book. The reliance upon this frequency is most key to our enlightenment. I hope that knowing this, you will have an easier time defining your expression of divine essence throughout eternity.

Prologue
ANDREA ELIZABETH — VISIONARY. SEER. WIFE. MOTHER. PSYCHIC. RECOVERING ALCOHOLIC.

I find it impossible to imagine my life being one of these six descriptions without the others. Each pivotal point assists the other, and each remedy or idea I have found is because I am one of these things. Having been to the bottom of my life, and worked my way upward and, more importantly, inward, I have at last found peace and a new way to live—free from all ideas of who I thought I was at any particular point in my life. Survival was my only mode for many years, until I surrendered and found that God, or my idea of God, was my threshold for my life.

I then began to recover, and discovered who I am. I found that I am a literal vibrational song of God, or Christ, or Christ-consciousness. I have found my place in the universal orchestra of life. I have found that deep down, I have found me. I resonate within my own vibration, within my own sound at my own level of understanding—first, who I am, and second, who God is.

I did not know much about God, only what my grandmothers had talked about, and since God was not much in my home, I believe it was easy for me to come to my own conclusions. So many people struggle with whether God is a man, or a woman, or a deity, or what-have-you. And since the beginning of time, either a religion or a God has molded our world, in every timeline, in every indigenous patriarchy, and in each of our family heritages. Many Native Americans were killed when the white men brought their bible here, trying to teach "their religion." So much death for something not really known.

In my 53 years here on this earth, I found no reason to read or watch movies about the idea of God. However, it has been shown to me many, many times recently as I write this book. I have simultaneously been given visions, seen the manuscript in my mind, as well as being told by my spiritual guides to write this book. I was led to various movies about priests who went to China to bring Christianity and were killed because of it, as well as the story of monks who kept their religion under wraps and lived in fear of being killed for believing in their God. I have been guided to watch movies about various ethnic groups who were killed in war zone areas in the name of God. I could literally go on forever, but I think my spirit guides wanted me to reinforce that God has been a main topic for centuries by teaching and writing about it as a culmination of time, religion, fear, lack, inferiority, hate, love, ad infinitum. God, I believe, will be a major topic from now into eternity, and my guides felt it important enough that I should reveal their thoughts through my writing, as well.

As a seer, I receive visions, I receive ideas, I see moving pictures in my mind's eye. I hear words, I hear music, I see future happenings, and I speak with various universal beings. At any given time, I am instructed to listen, sometimes by loud beeping in my ear, or perhaps a song will keep playing until I sit down and really listen to its meaning. I can be guided to a place, or to a name to research on Google, or I see a picture of an unusual insect to research. Ideas to brainstorm pop into my brain, a picture might appear, or a person and a connection. I work easily beyond the veil, I shall call it.

Having finally divulged a bit about who I am, I wish to bring to you, on a surreal spiritual level, a 21-day inner workings tool book for finding your inner substance, or God. Every word I type has its own visceral vibration, which means as I channel words from my guides, there are variances of vibratory sequences coming down from the universe, directing me to write these words that will be intentionally directed to those who need them. Together, you and I will begin to create a vibratory bond in which together we begin to heal, and to teach, and to learn how to become visionaries and masters of healing vibrations, as well as a vibratory source that is part of the universal soul. These words I bring forth have the capacity to rein your space into a semi-divulgent realm of facing yourself in order to become a more vibrant soul.

Each daily exercise assists you at a varying level, depending upon where you are vibrationally. Each word and each characterization of you elaborates a new beginning exactly where you are. You and I, WE begin to elaborate an enormous wave of insurmountable findings that have been hidden for so many years, or even for so many centuries, in your DNA. What will result from this work is whatever is required for you to overcome your past and allow yourself to begin creating a new future of self-recognition, self-appreciation, and self-acceptance. Love.

As one soul heals, the vibration that specific soul carries begins to ruminate and vibrate at such a healing rate that the person next to you cannot help but rise up to meet you where you are, not where they are. And as your own vibration continues to heal and to rise, everyone around you will do the same, unknowingly. I have been given the task of writing this book simply, easily, and methodically. Each chapter has its own flair and counterintuitive ideas.

Reading about God as if He is a man has many difficulties for some, as most people have been taught that God is something outside of themselves to pray to, or to honor. I also thought this was true. However, I now believe the opposite—that we are all God inside, or that we are God as an eternal vibration, and we can begin to change our thoughts on this and live as though we are God—in the flesh as a vibration. The definition I find most easy to understand is that we are the "essence of unconditional love expressed as light." That pretty much sums it up vibrationally, and takes away any label. I absolutely love this definition. So, as I write, I will not be writing the word God in terms of a deity or as one to behold as a man, I have been told to give God the name or definition for this work explained or expressed in terms of a vibration, or essence. In my channelings, I have been told to use the term the Holy Christed Being, and I will be writing as such. But, whatever works for you, make the idea of "God" something that you can trust and understand. As I am typing this, I am being shown a golden being or golden light, and the words Christ or Christed Being. And, as I am typing this, I am allowing the heavens above to ruminate light for all who are reading this book. I give to you on this particular day a look back into the time when our own religion kept you, or us, in the division of hate.

Now, I want to take you back even further into our galaxy explosion, or expansion, or birthing, or

Reading about God as if He is a man has many difficulties for some, as most people have been taught that God is something outside of themselves to pray to, or to honor. I also thought this was true. However, I now believe the opposite—that we are all God inside, or that we are God as an eternal vibration, and we can begin to change our thoughts on this and live as though we are God—in the flesh as a vibration. The definition I find most easy to understand is that we are the "essence of unconditional love expressed as light." That pretty much sums it up vibrationally, and takes away any label. I absolutely love this definition. So, as I write, I will not be writing the word God in terms of a deity or as one to behold as a man, I have been told to give God the name or definition for this work explained or expressed in terms of a vibration, or essence. In my channelings, I have been told to use the term the Holy Christed Being, and I will be writing as such. But, whatever works for you, make the idea of "God" something that you can trust and understand. As I am typing this, I am being shown a golden being or golden light, and the words Christ or Christed Being. And, as I am typing this, I am allowing the heavens above to ruminate light for all who are reading this book. I give to you on this particular day a look back into the time when our own religion kept you, or us, in the division of hate.

Now, I want to take you back even further into our galaxy explosion, or expansion, or birthing, or together we begin to heal, and to teach, and to learn how to become visionaries and masters of healing vibrations, as well as a vibratory source that is part of the universal soul. These words I bring forth have the capacity to rein your space into a semi-divulgent realm of facing yourself in order to become a more vibrant soul.

Each daily exercise assists you at a varying level, depending upon where you are vibrationally. Each word and each characterization of you elaborates a new beginning exactly where you are. You and I, WE begin to elaborate an enormous wave of insurmountable findings that have been hidden for so many years, or even for so many centuries, in your DNA. What will result from this work is whatever is required for you to overcome your past and allow yourself to begin creating a new future of self-recognition, self-appreciation, and self-acceptance. Love.

As one soul heals, the vibration that specific soul carries begins to ruminate and vibrate at such a healing rate that the person next to you cannot help but rise up to meet you where you are, not where they are. And as your own vibration continues to heal and to rise, everyone around you will do the same, unknowingly. I have been given the task of writing this book simply, easily, and methodically. Each chapter has its own flair and counterintuitive ideas.

whatever we "were." We were the idea of what was to come, and there was a vibration, or a vibrational pull, or a vibrational tug somewhere universally. That is what I am being told, and now I believe it to be true. I am also being told that this description or understanding is the very beginning of the Holy Christed Being Light. This light, this sound, this vision of life came from somewhere, but not from man, as man himself is disharmony, but the Christ Light or Christ Light Being is harmony. Perfection. The idea of the Holy Christed Being forming as a vibrational cadence or song for our life is magnificent, and this song is our own version of the Holy Christed Being magnificence in each of us. We have our own variance, as no one person is the same, just like our fingerprints. We are individual light beings, purposefully provided with just enough light and vibration to flourish for many, many lifetimes.

We can all speculate here and there what really happened before we were alive, but we all can at least agree that something happened out in space deep within the universal grid or matrix of our mere beginnings. If you think about this idea as universal, all things of matter are specific to the resonance or ratio of Pi, which is the mathematical calculation by man, of course, to signify perfection. I now believe this, mostly because the soul group of Sir Isaac Newton, Einstein, Plato, as well as Pythagoras have given me the opportunity to hear their words and write with and through them. I do not believe these men come to me in the form of men, but I believe that they come to me as frequency and that I somehow tapped into their own benevolence and their own fragment of themselves as frequency and vibration. As the universe speaks in vibrational resonance, I believe that is how I am able to hear them.

Chapter 1

Andrea Elizabeth — My Story

As an alcoholic joining AA for the 3rd time in my life, I did not expect to end up writing a book and speaking to God. I was a single mother working full time. I had 70 percent custody of my girls, Alexandria, 7, and Julia, 3, and I was going to school full time to become a paralegal. I was doing all of this my second year sober. I add this here because the work I did at the soul level through the 12 steps of AA and the 12 steps of Alanon gave me the practical idea of who God is in my life. The experience gave me the tools to live on a spiritual platform, believing in a God that I was able to comprehend. In addition, I was able to critically form a bond with this God of my understanding, and I quickly learned that I needed some type of belief, or power. I needed to believe in something other than myself—something in which I could turn over my own will, trusting that this power was the key to living sober, free, and without fear.

In so doing, I managed to create, unknowingly, a deep resounding force within me that re-opened my galaxy to the stars, and I became free from my own inner dragons. I cleared my life of garbage and hate, distrust, abuse, being abusive, and alcohol. I did what is called a 4th step, which made me take responsibility for every wrong or hurtful thing I had ever done to anyone. I wrote down my resentments, fears, sexual misconduct, and other harmful behaviors toward others and their causes, as well. But most importantly, I was able to see and take responsibility for my own actions—the good, the bad, and the ugly. I got to see my life on paper, written in terms of my old ideas and behaviors, and my ridiculed existence. I belatedly saw that my life was being run on self-will, fear, selfishness, fright, hatred, disobedience to myself and to God. I was made to take full responsibility for my actions and to make amends to those I had harmed, and to clear the air about my life with others. Human relationships are difficult when one is selfish. It is basically a one-way street: my way or the highway.

At the same time, I realized I'd been living my life enmeshed in the "7 Deadly Sins"—Pride, Anger, Greed, Gluttony, Lust, Envy, and Sloth. I had the primal self-centered fear, losing things I believed I possessed, or not getting things I believed I wanted. Although living as a child in a grown-up body, I was being manipulated by the strings of fear and anger attached to all these human failings.

As I confessed my human sins to another human being, I felt so absolutely relieved of all the emotions, the fear, the hate, and the secrets I had held onto for my entire lifetime. I was 34 at the time, and I had a boatload of secrets. In sharing this in a "confession" setting, I felt relief for the first time in my life. I was comfortable in my skin and, most importantly, after sharing that, I had a vision, and I felt the presence of God. It felt so comforting and real that I wanted more. But that didn't happen. So, realizing that I could not keep confessing, since I had already cleared away the "garbage" I had been carrying, I felt inclined to begin sitting and praying for longer periods of time, asking for guidance, listening, and then seeing the things that I had "asked" for begin to occur. I began to form a real or true relationship with a God of my understanding. More importantly, I found a book called *The Sermon on the Mount: The Key to Success in Life* (1934), ISBN 0-06-062862-6. Although this book is very Christian in some parts, I was able to get around all that and use the book as a tool for my enlightenment.

The book had little tricks and exercises in it, and I read it over and over for many years. And what I found was that "if thine eye be single, thy body shall be full of light." At first I didn't get that statement, but as I began to sit and meditate with my consciousness in my 3rd chakra, or my upper belly, and repeat to myself: "Be still, and know that I am God," over and over for some years. Finally, I felt this presence, and I felt this light beginning to ignite deep within. Over time, I discovered that no religion, or priest, or pastor could give this to me. I had to find it for myself, and in the end I found that, yes, I am God, or Christ, or source, or the universe—I am all of these inside. The more I practiced the opposite of those human failings, I found I began practicing more of and living in the characteristics of God.

For lack of better terms, I came to live in the simple ideology of purity, charity, unselfishness, and love—the four absolutes of the AA program. I also began living in the spiritual principles behind the 12 steps—honesty, hope, faith, courage, integrity, willingness, humility, brotherly love, discipline, perseverance, awareness, and service. As I untrained myself out of the old, and retrained myself into the new, I felt a sense of serenity and peace I had never known. The more I acted the new way and practiced living in these new characteristics of God, my life began to get lighter and lighter, and the more I began to trust that whatever I needed would be provided. I began to have trust in the universe. I outgrew the fear I had lived with my entire life and began to live in trust. The more I trusted, the more inner peace I had, and the more inner peace I had, the lighter I began to feel. I began journaling during my first year and practiced writing letters to God. I thanked Him for my sobriety, and started living in gratitude for all things that had happened—good and bad.

over for some years. Finally, I felt this presence, and I felt this light beginning to ignite deep within. Over time, I discovered that no religion, or priest, or pastor could give this to me. I had to find it for myself, and in the end I found that, yes, I am God, or Christ, or source, or the universe—I am all of these inside. The more I practiced the opposite of those human failings, I found I began practicing more of and living in the characteristics of God.

For lack of better terms, I came to live in the simple ideology of purity, charity, unselfishness, and love—the four absolutes of the AA program. I also began living in the spiritual principles behind the 12 steps—honesty, hope, faith, courage, integrity, willingness, humility, brotherly love, discipline, perseverance, awareness, and service. As I untrained myself out of the old, and retrained myself into the new, I felt a sense of serenity and peace I had never known. The more I acted the new way and practiced living in these new characteristics of God, my life began to get lighter and lighter, and the more I began to trust that whatever I needed would be provided. I began to have trust in the universe. I outgrew the fear I had lived with my entire life and began to live in trust. The more I trusted, the more inner peace I had, and the more inner peace I had, the lighter I began to feel. I began journaling during my first year and practiced writing letters to God. I thanked Him for my sobriety, and started living in gratitude for all things that had happened—good and bad.

As I confessed my human sins to another human being, I felt so absolutely relieved of all the emotions, the fear, the hate, and the secrets I had held onto for my entire lifetime. I was 34 at the time, and I had a boatload of secrets. In sharing this in a "confession" setting, I felt relief for the first time in my life. I was comfortable in my skin and, most importantly, after sharing that, I had a vision, and I felt the presence of God. It felt so comforting and real that I wanted more. But that didn't happen. So, realizing that I could not keep confessing, since I had already cleared away the "garbage" I had been carrying, I felt inclined to begin sitting and praying for longer periods of time, asking for guidance, listening, and then seeing the things that I had "asked" for begin to occur. I began to form a real or true relationship with a God of my understanding. More importantly, I found a book called *The Sermon on the Mount: The Key to Success in Life* (1934), ISBN 0-06-062862-6. Although this book is very Christian in some parts, I was able to get around all that and use the book as a tool for my enlightenment.

The book had little tricks and exercises in it, and I read it over and over for many years. And what I found was that "if thine eye be single, thy body shall be full of light." At first I didn't get that statement, but as I began to sit and meditate with my consciousness in my 3rd chakra, or my upper belly, and repeat to myself: "Be still, and know that I am God," over and

Andrea's Reiki Story

Fast forward to 2012, when I was attuned to Reiki, and my life changed forever. Reiki is an ancient Japanese energy healing technique in which you work with the universal life force energy to heal yourself and others. After my first Reiki attunement, I began to see moving pictures in my left eye, and I started knowing things about people that they had not told me. The more open I got within, the more universally knowledgeable I became. Today I know that this power or vibration has been with me my entire life. And being an open channel as God for God, I believe my clarity allowed me to become an open forum for the universe to begin speaking, and for me to begin listening.

What to do with all of this?

As a seer, I am a channeler, which means that I receive messages from spirit, or universe, or whoever vibrationally wishes to have words. Some messages and information may be from past historically significant people and are actually frequencies that I pick up. These frequencies are also people who have passed on and have some type of unresolved issues they feel need to be addressed. In this work, I am able to help settle unresolved issues and grief, and I serve as a bridge from the dead to the living. Now this is not what I signed up for, but I have begun to live with it, because the people are very grateful to receive healing and closure for their grief. I add all this so that you will know where I came from, and why I am writing this book.

While in Australia in February of 2018, my guides told me that I would be writing a book and that it would be a 21-day workbook and prayer book, and that it would be called "What if You were God?" They told me it would carry my vibratory energy in each and every word in order to help readers to heal, and allow them to master their own human frailties within. The vibration of each and every word has a masterly devout calling to your soul. I am told that each word will enhance your being in ways I don't even know yet. And, as you continue to read, and work through your human failings, remember to jot down some ideas and share them with me so that I can know I am on the right path. This is not a singlehanded life we are living—we are all ONE universally. My website is: www.beurownreligion.com, and the tab is "What if You were God?" I invite you to share any ideas you may have for helping humanity with me and our community. Please join our Facebook community, "Be Your Own Religion" at https://www.facebook.com/andreaelizabeth2020/ and become part of something bigger.

We are all in this together, and "ain't no one getting out alive." So why not try something new? Give yourself the chance to heal, get to better know your inner self, and allow magic in your life every day. There are no guarantees that you will believe what I say, but I write anyway—for the non-believers as well as the believers. There has to be something more, right? I am guided each and every day to sit and type for us. I do not write this for me, I am a channel for each and every person reading this right now. I feel you, I know you, and I honor you. Blessed be. Let's get ready to change.

I thank each and every one of you for allowing me to be of service to the universe in this capacity to honor my own inner Holy Christed Being (HCB), and yours.

Finally, as I add this writing, each of you reading this book also will have a vibrational input. Along with Master Jesus, our Holy Blessed Mother, Master Buddha, Divine Master Kwan Yin, Archangel Michael, Master Sir Lento, any and all of the Ascended Masters, Nostradamus, Plato, Pythagoras, Einstein, Sir Isaac Newton, King Arthur and The Knights of the Round Table, and all benevolent beings abound. This is not my book, this is OUR book. I thank each and every being who reads these words, and I am enamored at your light as I see you.

Namaste.

Chapter 2
The Untrusting Soul Space

I have been told to write this piece from the standpoint of an Untrusting Soul Space, the fully laden soul space, and the unnatural trusting space for those who are in need of some soul enlightenment and to use their disillusionment voice. This is written for you and by you, as together we all heal.

If you are feeling lost in your soul reside, then this is the place to begin. If you are listless, restless, discontented and feel undeserving, then you have found the safe place of your reside. In this space, I write solely from a place of the un-divine, but it will take you to the place of the divine. If you wish, you do not have to travel with us, but you can read and see what these formed words do for your soul's space. Even a bit of trust may come and give way for you to ascertain your love of God, from your soul deep within, so that you may begin to hold trust for your own soul. We now begin.

Prayer 1: The Torch of the Unsought Soul
Dear Spirit,
We ask on this day as we bring in together the pure, raw, and unidentified parts of our soul. We ask deeply from our heart space where it is pure and full of love that we begin to open a tiny crevice from within, so as to begin singing a new revolutionary song of our soul.. Within this pure resonance, we ask to be able to persevere along with Andrea Elizabeth for these next 21 days of life-changing and life-giving insight brought to each of us by spirits deeply held within our holy and devout space. As we bring together this time and space, we are creating for a grand reception for our soul as we step past the old lingering threshold of fear and into a new trusting space of grace, forgiveness, and magic.
Amen

This magic space will open new avenues by creating new visions of you by asking new questions, such as: How do I wish to live today? What kind of light do I wish to carry today? How can I live free today? How can I make my soul shine today?

You will switch from a future living space to a daily living space. You will begin living in the NOW. Our Hope for you is that you will begin to master yourself so that there will be a new design in your life of fun, delight, peace, grace, and solace. A new you is in the making.

My Army of Spiritual Assistants

I do wish to add that in the writing of this book, I write with an army of assistants. Some I have mentioned above, and others come around in a time of need of an energetic boost or an angelic word, or a fairy tale that needs to be inserted. As you begin to read these words, some may seem privy only to the holy or educated but, believe me, I am neither of these things. I have to look up so many of the words I type to find their meaning, and in doing so I do my best to try not to change the words that I am given via channeling. This may also challenge you to find a dictionary and learn these new words with me, as I can honestly tell you that half of these words are foreign to me. But as I write them and look them up, they fit perfectly as I have written them. This work is so amazing, and I am honored to share it with each of you.

As we gather our hearts, minds, and desires, we design from a space of "inner-continental divide" and we co-manufacture from a space of displacement of our peace. WE are going to begin to really feel and become malleable inside so as to begin wondering from the inside of our soul to the outside of our mind where our soul and our spiritual matrix are in a division. This, I believe, is the perfect working space for us to begin.

At times of duty, we so often regulate our minds from a space of unnatural surroundings, and cultivate from a space of happenstance. We do not

My Army of Spiritual Assistants

I do wish to add that in the writing of this book, I write with an army of assistants. Some I have mentioned above, and others come around in a time of need of an energetic boost or an angelic word, or a fairy tale that needs to be inserted. As you begin to read these words, some may seem privy only to the holy or educated but, believe me, I am neither of these things. I have to look up so many of the words I type to find their meaning, and in doing so I do my best to try not to change the words that I am given via channeling. This may also challenge you to find a dictionary and learn these new words with me, as I can honestly tell you that half of these words are foreign to me. But as I write them and look them up, they fit perfectly as I have written them. This work is so amazing, and I am honored to share it with each of you.

As we gather our hearts, minds, and desires, we design from a space of "inner-continental divide" and we co-manufacture from a space of displacement of our peace. WE are going to begin to really feel and become malleable inside so as to begin wondering from the inside of our soul to the outside of our mind where our soul and our spiritual matrix are in a division. This, I believe, is the perfect working space for us to begin.

At times of duty, we so often regulate our minds from a space of unnatural surroundings, and cultivate from a space of happenstance. We do not

Prayer 1: The Torch of the Unsought Soul
Dear Spirit,
We ask on this day as we bring in together the pure, raw, and unidentified parts of our soul. We ask deeply from our heart space where it is pure and full of love that we begin to open a tiny crevice from within, so as to begin singing a new revolutionary song of our soul.. Within this pure resonance, we ask to be able to persevere along with Andrea Elizabeth for these next 21 days of life-changing and life-giving insight brought to each of us by spirits deeply held within our holy and devout space. As we bring together this time and space, we are creating for a grand reception for our soul as we step past the old lingering threshold of fear and into a new trusting space of grace, forgiveness, and magic.
Amen

This magic space will open new avenues by creating new visions of you by asking new questions, such as: How do I wish to live today? What kind of light do I wish to carry today? How can I live free today? How can I make my soul shine today?

You will switch from a future living space to a daily living space. You will begin living in the NOW. Our Hope for you is that you will begin to master yourself so that there will be a new design in your life of fun, delight, peace, grace, and solace. A new you is in the making.

create our own space. We follow along the ways others demonstrate. And, however much we may wish to do so, we cannot measure up to those or others' expectations of our own life. We ultimately decide who we are at any given time, based upon others' actuality for us. In doing so, we cultivate our soul from a space of disbelief rather than belief. We view life from a fractured point of view of how others view us, as well as how we view ourselves through the eyes of another. We ultimately derive the following conclusion of our space: We regularly deny our own soul its right to be safe. The lesson in this is that if we are not safe, we are not in trust. Period.

And, how is this even possible? Well, the list can go on and on, but we will naturally forbid the right choices or make wrong decisions, and the heavens seemingly deny us good. Or so we think. In reality, we deny our own good. If we feel we are not responsible enough, or deserving enough, or actionable enough, we deny our truth. And by living in the untruth, we live in the actuality of the untruth and we live in a false existence.

To live in an actionable space, we intentionally need to live this following divine premise.

As I wake, I trust that my divine soul is no longer lifeless, but is filled with love, attention, and delight. These words kindly describe how well we can feel and live today. And if we actuate each and every day, fully, vibrantly, and decidedly, in and through the divine, we shall be free. We will no longer have to be a caged soul. Our doors will be opened, and our journey will begin.

A Formidable Beginning

In the beginning stages of soul-targeting, we must ascertain particular aspects of a trusting soul, how to react, and act as if we are already trust. It is a matter of un-doing and then re-doing, or un-acting and then re-acting differently.

As we begin this journey of trust together, we activate an openness between the two of us that cultivates a trust within us both, and I know as you are working within this space, your openness will divulge great secrets about yourself that you have never really perceived before. Your plan will now become a plan for your soul. Take a good look at this plan when you are finished with this book, as it is a soul plan or a life plan for your soul.

Just know that each and every time you shudder at a topic I suggest, you must simply know it is an untruth and needs to be looked at. Pay very close attention to these aspects of yourself, notice how each topic makes you feel in your mind, body, and soul, because this is where the trickster hidden in you will begin to open up and be exposed. Always know that in these workings, you will fully and presently reside here, now, and within your own deepest knowing of your truth and ultimately within your soul reside. Stay deeply intertwined within as you write these untruths about yourself so that you can see the so-called trickery of your soul space.

This is a 21-day soul-activating, soul-stimulating journal for you to write in and co-create future goals. As you progress each day, write a goal you would like to complete for yourself, and by the end of 21 days, you will have a soul life plan.

Give it a go, and have yourself a good time with it. There are no right or wrong answers here, as this will be YOUR journal of YOUR truth and the truth of YOUR soul. Imagine the possibilities when you trust your soul! The journey of a lifetime is beginning here now. This is a special manifestation space that has been opened specifically for you to work in. When you are finished each day and close your journal, this healing space closes. Each time you open your journal, it's as though magic appears in your space once again, and as you begin using your magic wand, aka your pen, you begin manifesting magic once again in this journal.

As you are writing in this journal, imagine you are creating a masterpiece of your soul and that your magic wand is the creator of magic. Allow in the flow of the angels and guides to come forth and be strong in your words. Together, as we read and think about each and every word we write, each and every word brings in the energy of our own creation. You are literally recreating your life each and every time you journal. Thoughts and words are energy, and as they are spoken or written, they create mass. Together we are co-creating anything and everything you wish for, as protectively and as honorably and as openly as possible. Dream Big, Write Big, and Create Big! Godspeed!

At The Beginning of Each Day
You want to begin each day with a new, clear, open space. Preface that with a look at the previous day's pages in order to realign yourself with the stronghold of the peace of your soul.

Next, you want to create a design space that works for you. As for most people, a simple space may or may not do. You will get the hang of it, don't fret!

Adhere to a very proclivital writing space where you can simply jot down your untruths so that they can be changed and become your real soul-truths. Each and every day, imagine a specific region of the heart to work from and then magnify this area with some sort of cataclysmic desire for life, or simply see your heart space light up like a candle and begin from there.

Dive into a space for the untold to become the told, the real to become the real, and the magical science to be unleashed.

I write this 21-day book for those who seek to change. I support you, and I support your journey to your soul and finding your inner substance.
Blessings,
Andrea Elizabeth

Chapter 3

Day 1 – Peeking Inside Our Truth

Prayer 2: My Prayer for Self Truths
On this first day, I ask that I am able to fortify my space so that I shall be open just enough to peek inside my truth.

Truths About Ourselves

Truths about ourselves could be our family truths, family design, family religion, family ideas, family functions and dysfunctions—all creating the makeup of our human design and any idea or truth about us that came from our family of origin. Many of our truths, or "untruths," come from our family line and other relationships along the way. Whatever their beliefs were about themselves were passed down to us as children, and we took on those same beliefs about ourselves.

As we get older and act upon what we have been taught, the truths about ourselves change, depending on our actions, inactions, and reactions. There are so many things about ourselves that we are confused about, or do not even know where they came from.

We are writing today about any and all realized self-truths that keep us unsafe, and in our non-truth. We use this as a reference tool to find out what keeps us in misalignment with our soul.

We will keep it easy this day and begin with the first 5 or more untruths of who we are, based upon our past. Feel free to write openly, either more or less.

As you state this and every other prayer written in this book, always begin with imagining a bubble, with us together in it. That way we are intertwined, guided, and in relation to one another, allowing in the magic of freedom.

Let's state together, and really hear my voice as we state this "Freedom of Truth" prayer. (You can listen and speak together with me on this daily prayer at www.beurownreligion/What if you were God? / Prayer 3.) When you are comfortable and ready state the following:

Prayer 3: Prayer of Freedom
I, together with Andrea Elizabeth, coincide with her spirit's voice to allow freedom into my space for all eternity. In opening this new space and allowing in this wonder of delight, we activate together and participate in the realm of true forgiveness and light. And as we cut the cosmic tie of the untruth of our self, we together mend the ways of my life as all is well in the beginning, and all will be well in the end. So be it.

so many things about ourselves that we are confused about, or do not even know where they came from.

We are writing today about any and all realized self-truths that keep us unsafe, and in our non-truth. We use this as a reference tool to find out what keeps us in misalignment with our soul.

We will keep it easy this day and begin with the first 5 or more untruths of who we are, based upon our past. Feel free to write openly, either more or less.

As you state this and every other prayer written in this book, always begin with imagining a bubble, with us together in it. That way we are intertwined, guided, and in relation to one another, allowing in the magic of freedom.

Let's state together, and really hear my voice as we state this "Freedom of Truth" prayer. (You can listen and speak together with me on this daily prayer at www.beurownreligion/What if you were God? / Prayer 3.) When you are comfortable and ready state the following:

Prayer 3: Prayer of Freedom
I, together with Andrea Elizabeth, coincide with her spirit's voice to allow freedom into my space for all eternity. In opening this new space and allowing in this wonder of delight, we activate together and participate in the realm of true forgiveness and light. And as we cut the cosmic tie of the untruth of our self, we together mend the ways of my life as all is well in the beginning, and all will be well in the end. So be it.

Chapter 3
Day 1 – Peeking Inside Our Truth

Prayer 2: My Prayer for Self Truths
On this first day, I ask that I am able to fortify my space so that I shall be open just enough to peek inside my truth.

Truths About Ourselves

Truths about ourselves could be our family truths, family design, family religion, family ideas, family functions and dysfunctions—all creating the makeup of our human design and any idea or truth about us that came from our family of origin. Many of our truths, or "untruths," come from our family line and other relationships along the way. Whatever their beliefs were about themselves were passed down to us as children, and we took on those same beliefs about ourselves.

As we get older and act upon what we have been taught, the truths about ourselves change, depending on our actions, inactions, and reactions. There are

My Untruths:
Here are a few examples of what my untruths are,
or what I believe to be true about myself:

- I am the black sheep because I do not work at a job that my family wishes for me.
- I am a Catholic, Protestant, Jew, Muslim. I have been ridiculed for my beliefs in the past, and I have trouble with God.
- I am dumb. I have been told by my father that I am dumb and need to be married, because I will never make it on my own.
- I did not go to college like my brother, and therefore I am irresponsible.
- I have been bullied at school or at home, and have been called fat, ugly, dumb, or stupid.
- I am a terrible housekeeper because my house is not like my mother's house.
- I am a bad person, and I was told I deserved to be abused.

Here I try to give examples of what other people's ideas or truths about us are and, after living in these ideas and untruths, we begin to believe they are OUR real truth. But, they are neither our truths nor the truth of our soul; they are the untruths that keep our soul hidden, because we are living someone else's truth about us.

I don't know how many times prior to my awakening and finding out about who I really am, I lived my life based upon what my family thought I should do or be. I stayed in a marriage of untruth for 12 years because my family told me to. They said things like, "He is a good provider and you do not want other men in the house with your children" (which is good advice, by the way); or, "No one will want a woman with two children," or when I was 24, they would ask me, "Why don't you have any children yet? I want grandchildren. You are not getting any younger." My point here is that our young lives are based upon so many untruths from our family of origin, or who we are raised by—other people's ideas of who we should be. I include this first to find out who we are not. That way, we can find out who we are. List of 5 Current Untruths About Me:

1)

2)

3)

4)

5)

Which one of these five untruths stand out the most in your real vision of you? Why?

Really get to the crux of this untruth, as this will set the tone of your journey for the next 21 days; it takes 21 days to break a habit. So let's make these days count.

If you wish, write a paragraph about your own untruth, and bring us together in your space. We can commingle our energies to become fruitful in our journey on this road together in spirit. You can always call on me and allow me into your working space. This is not a collegiate battle of wits; this is a life-long, triumphant journey to your soul. Don't worry, you won't be latching on to me energetically. I have opened up a spiritual container space for this book. All ideas, graces, strongholds of ideas that people bring here are put into a bubble of light, and shifted back out into the universe to be healed. Our purpose is for the person working in this book to find peace and begin to understand who they are as a person, as a human, and as a soul. This spiritual container is available for everyone to access when feeling confused, unsure, sad, or lost in the words here. Simply connect to this container by imaging it in your mind's eye and creating a bridge to it. It is a simple connection. Then simply pray and ask for guidance. It will come, I promise! The helpers here have been using such a container for centuries. This is not something I have created. I am just connecting you with the spiritual realm so that you, too, can be convinced of your greatness.

Please use these tools. I have channeled them for you as a way out of the earthbound existence, so you can live free within and have a real understanding of your living truth—the real truth of who you are and what you are about. That way, you will no longer be tied to your earthbound body, but living from and creating deeply within to begin your soul's new adventure. How exciting for you, for us! I believe that as one soul clears and understands their self, the frequency of the planet begins to rise just a little bit more and humanity benefits. As one person begins healing so do others, that is the real magic of this work and service to our planet.

Let's do this together for the next 21 days to really find out about who you were, and re-establish who you are now. You will confront many aspects of yourself during these 21 days and, as encouragement, we all, together as one, will bring hope and deep affection for the inner workings of your soul-based journey. You will not be disappointed in the outcome, as you will find yourself and begin to manage your soul based upon you and no other person, in particular, the old you, inherently.

Our goal here on this first day is to predict your soul's future as to which way is up, so to speak. We will indelibly coincide with your truths, your untruths and your specificity of Christ, or God, or light, Allah or source. Whichever chord or name or vision you choose to work toward is your choice. You may use the words Essence of Unconditional Love Expressed as Light if you wish.

This fantastic 21-day goal-setting book is soulfully dramatized to create a new song for your reality, allowing you to become strong enough inside to have insight for the outside and to begin living a life of true, open-love kinship with us, the angels, the ascended masters and your fellow earth-beings. We are all a nation of ONE, yet we have forgotten our purpose. And I bring this information to you, to find your truth.

On this day 1, let us open your heart, your earthly mind, and your fragmented soul to the brink of its existence, and allow the old insanity to rise up, be cleared out of your infested heart, mind, and soul space, and consign a newness into your soul to live free. Blessings to all who come to this place of resistance, as you have found the correct space to begin. Blessed be.

Prayer 4: Prayer of Allowing

I allow on this day 1 of our journey together, the light of forgiveness, the love of my truth, and the adherence to grace in our work. I now ascertain God's grace in my space. May the peace and joy of togetherness be strong as we walk on this journey of oneness together.

Fill in the page with any and all ideas that come to mind, for you have opened up the magical bubble of light. Stay in this magical bubble as long as you like; persist as much as you can, then close the magical bubble of light without any judgment.

My Day 1 Goal for my soul: I will assist you with the first day.

My Day 1 Soul Goal: To be free in living my own truth

Thought for the day:

Today I live within my freedom and the vigor of my truth. May I live this way forevermore.

Chapter 4
DAY 2 – WILLINGNESS TO CHANGE

An abundance of greatness is to be had by those who are granted freedom from themselves. Today, as we open up our bubble working space together, we will pacify those untruths of yesterday and create a new space to endeavor. What this means exactly is that our openness creates space for a newness of cause in our lives, and we coexistently create from afar. Essentially, we derive the new from the old, and, for the most part, the old parts of us will die off and the new parts will take over as trust and safety in your own soul space. For the alliance to take place all at once, we together, in this space of luxury, deem the following statement:

Willingness Statement

In actuality, on this day, if I find that all my life has been a lie to myself, my reality has been askew. From this point forward, I ask for the forgiveness space to be further widened as Andrea Elizabeth and I cultivate

Chapter 4

DAY 2 – WILLINGNESS TO CHANGE

An abundance of greatness is to be had by those who are granted freedom from themselves. Today, as we open up our bubble working space together, we will pacify those untruths of yesterday and create a new space to endeavor. What this means exactly is that our openness creates space for a newness of cause in our lives, and we coexistently create from afar. Essentially, we derive the new from the old, and, for the most part, the old parts of us will die off and the new parts will take over as trust and safety in your own soul space. For the alliance to take place all at once, we together, in this space of luxury, deem the following statement:

Willingness Statement

In actuality, on this day, if I find that all my life has been a lie to myself, my reality has been askew. From this point forward, I ask for the forgiveness space to be further widened as Andrea Elizabeth and I cultivate are all a nation of ONE, yet we have forgotten our purpose. And I bring this information to you, to find your truth.

On this day 1, let us open your heart, your earthly mind, and your fragmented soul to the brink of its existence, and allow the old insanity to rise up, be cleared out of your infested heart, mind, and soul space, and consign a newness into your soul to live free. Blessings to all who come to this place of resistance, as you have found the correct space to begin. Blessed be.

Prayer 4: Prayer of Allowing

I allow on this day 1 of our journey together, the light of forgiveness, the love of my truth, and the adherence to grace in our work. I now ascertain God's grace in my space. May the peace and joy of togetherness be strong as we walk on this journey of oneness together.

Fill in the page with any and all ideas that come to mind, for you have opened up the magical bubble of light. Stay in this magical bubble as long as you like; persist as much as you can, then close the magical bubble of light without any judgment.

My Day 1 Goal for my soul: I will assist you with the first day.

My Day 1 Soul Goal: To be free in living my own truth

Thought for the day:
Today I live within my freedom and the vigor of my truth. May I live this way forevermore.

a new devotional space for grace, even further than yesterday. Today, we open this space with pure love, enjoyment, and tactful support of each other. And we hold each other up, especially when the other is a bit down or under the weather. Forming this partnership creates further mastership for me and, in doing so, I am able to coexist with Andrea Elizabeth in her space and in her magic. We now fully open up a space of wonder to work in on this day 2.

The work for this day is fully exuberating and brings power within your willfulness to change.

Questions

Ask yourself this question:

How much do I wish to change my soul space? Pick a number from 1 to 21.

This will begin to form an alliance between you, your soul, as the number you pick will be the pace at which you work. So choose wisely.

Willingness to change my soul space? _____

Now, with this number in mind, how can you actuate your relevance about your willingness to change? In other words, how can you fully envelop your own soul's space to actively want to be in charge of your life?

With this number in mind, let's take a step back and see how the number coincides with your life now. Is it a low number? Does the number assimilate your current lifestyle? Do you feel less than, or have depression, or anxiety, or the like? Or is it a high number with very high expectations of yourself that you never seem to be able to attain?

I do this exercise to show that if we try to keep tabs on ourselves as a sort of judgment, we are literally failing before we begin. If we just simply trust that this process will work, then our work will be truthful and easy. Sorry for the trickery, but I had to give you the right picture so that you would try not to project the rest of the time in this journey. We want to stay present in this particular day and stay focused on this particular path.

Prayer 5: Daily Togetherness in Partnership Prayer

Today as I, together with Andrea Elizabeth, open up a space to gather my thoughts of unworthiness about myself, and we actuate in terms of privity of our own secrets. We indulge in frequent forgiveness of ourselves, our old judgements of ourselves, and our old energy. We now ask that the presence of forgiveness be our ground layer to build upon with grace, mercy, dignity, and truth. We hold back nothing in opening up our light so that we may commit to change.

Our Secrets

What are my greatest secrets that I keep from my past and not one person even knows about? (Don't worry, I won't tap in and see or know them.) These secrets keep you imprisoned in your own perceived jail. They can be real events that have happened to us, or even things made up by our own psyche that keep us imprisoned.

Really sit with this one a bit, and allow the magic together to clear up a space of doubt in your own soul. As we clear these secrets, we open up a space in our souls for more sadness to be let out, and for more forgiveness and grace to be allowed in. Let's list up to 10 secrets. If you don't have that many, it doesn't matter. If there are more, then write more. It doesn't matter; this is YOUR work, not anyone else's to know about, or see.

My Secrets:

1)

2)

3)

4)

5)

6)

7)

8)

9)

10)

A Word About Our Secrets

What I wish to write about our secrets is that each one we keep, be it good or bad, silences a little part of our heart and soul. It sort of locks a door to solace that we once had. In opening up this door of lies, untruths and deceits, and/or abuse that we have either done to others or have had done to us, we give up a piece of the past in order to allow our future light to come in. Be as open and as honest as you may, because only you will reap the benefits of this work.

Godspeed!

Day 2 Soul Goal is: to live free in my heart and soul

Thought for the day:

Today, I live free from my past. I am no longer imprisoned. May I live this way forevermore. Today, may I be an open book for myself to live in wonder and awe always.

Chapter 5

Day 3 – Self-Deception to Truth With the Australian Aboriginals

Prayer 6: Daily Togetherness in Partnership Prayer
Today, we ask that I am guarded against spiritual unrest, and allow Andrea Elizabeth and myself to bring forth the untold manufactured lies I have told myself my entire life. Allow me to have access to the dire need for forgiveness, as I once was a free soul.

On this day, I unlock a little more of my soul space so that I may allow in the conglomerated space of sheer delight that many share. In many ways these lies keep me bound to the desperate need for silence. After today, I never have to be silent again, as I regain a new thought process of design for tranquility and soul alliance in God's truth. Today I pray it shall be granted that all manufactured lies I have created are withdrawn—fruitless now and forevermore. So be it!

Today's journey is based upon our own illicit space. Where we created lies to justify our thinking, our behavior, or our actions. We cultivate insecurity or instability in our own lives as we do this. Today we will find in our soul space any and all manufactured lies that we all say to ourselves so that we do not have to take any action, so that we do not have to engage with ourselves or others, or so that the daily manufactured grind can go on without us. Today we write together, with the speed of lightning, our own sort of characteristics of our plight, or the untruths of our souls.

List up to 10 manufactured lies you state to yourself in order to feel comfortable in your own skin. For instance, how many doughnuts did I eat, a dozen, or 6? Or, I really didn't drink that many beers; I only drank half the pack. Actually, I drank the full pack. The justification of our actions in our own minds keeps us in a state of undesired status, if you will. The lies we create from within nullify our own greatness. How can we ever free ourselves from such self-deception if we do not face our truth? This keeps us from our greatness and our freedom. Write about the manufactured lies that are current in your life. You can add more later.

List up to 10 manufactured lies here, and ask yourself why you do this. Let's take a look at why you seem to justify the lies in your own mind. What do you really seem to gain from that justification?

1)
2)
3)
4)
5)
6)
7)
8)
9)
10)

What this will show us are the ways in which we have created untruths in our own lives, the horror we anticipate, and the deranged lives we lead because of it. This is very deep work of self-rationalization.

Andrea Elizabeth side note:
I am astounded each day I sit down to write at what comes out on the computer. Today I am writing from Terrigal, on the Central Coast of New South Wales, about 35 kilometers north of Sydney. Each time I travel, I am delighted at the energetic presence that comes and writes with me during my trips. So this work is written for you with a huge Aboriginal presence. Be it known that you are not just working with Andrea Elizabeth, you are currently working with the divine presence of, and within, the Aboriginal people and the loveliness and tenderness in their hearts and souls. Bringing forth their ancient wisdom and healing abilities by me, and through me.

As soon as we touched down in Sydney from Melbourne, I immediately felt the softness of the hearts of the animals, such as the koalas and the kangaroos, and I was astonished by the love that came deep into my heart. I felt the softness of the animals and the softness of the love and kindness of the people.

So please know that these words have come from the highest places in vibration, the deepest in love and kindness, and the most real that have ever been written in this modern-day presence.

My Day 3 Soul Goal is:
Thought for the day:
Today I am honest with myself. May I live this way forevermore.

Chapter 6
Day 4 – Accomplishments

Let's take a look back at our accomplishments so far. We have noticed a few untruths, distrusts, and manufactured lies, which required taking an honest look at ourselves from a perspective of grief, I believe. As we change, at some point we must begin to miss some part of ourselves, don't you think?

In grieving, I have found that small parts of our journey have been hindered somewhat by such grief of the loss of our souls. And in this bereavement space, we can undoubtedly feel some unkind things about ourselves.

Today let's take a look at the grieving part of our souls—the misunderstanding, misalignment, and mistreated emotions that have led up to this point. Our grieving souls are amiss with a culture of almost hate sometimes; for example, if we are a bit emotional, others say suck it up, or be a man, or get over it!

Emotions, feelings, and truths are not going to move along easily. Each and every emotion and feeling has an emotional charge, an energy that affects us in some way, usually misaligning our soul with a sort of off-space, if you will. We all have an energy packet here, and each emotional charge either puts us on or off this path. What I am being shown is that the grief energetic charge seems to hinder us the most. And isn't it funny, because we are all born to die, yet the worst energetic emotional charge is death, or loss.

Today, let's write about our loss energy, or bereavement energy. You can break it down as: loss of anything that we have had in our possession, or felt, was ours but was taken away, and then left an energetic hole inside. As I write this, it seems they're the same category, as loss and bereavement are the same thing—one is a loss, a sort of hole that is left, and bereavement is the energy that has been overtaken from the loss. So whichever way or whichever term you wish to use, let's write about the loss space in your soul.

We write these losses from a place of hurt and regret, so do not be hard on yourself it is difficult at first. The more you endure the pain and step into the unity and healing aspect of this exercise, the more your soul will become willing to change.

Examples:

List up to 10 Main Losses or Bereavements in Your Life:

1)

2)

3)

4)

5)

6)

7)

8)

9

10)

When this list is complete and the pain has welled up in your tears, recite the following prayer.

Prayer 7: Daily Togetherness in Partnership Prayer
Today, as I, together with the Aboriginal Elders and Andrea Elizabeth, fully and wholeheartedly give myself the ability to ascertain a new enlightenment deep within, I allow others to heal as well, as I cut the ties of hate, of resentment, of hurt, of the pain of deep, manufactured self-illness. I have held this pain and difficulty long enough. As I begin cutting this tie, the cosmic loop of pain is untied, and I am set free from deep inside my soul space. Blessed be!

Heavenly Mother wishes words:
Andrea Elizabeth and I, on this great day of astonishment, wish to form a great bond with your soul space that soars within. Within your deepness

and in your cataclysmic space of turmoil, we identify your pain and wish it to be relieved gently, kindly, and in great solace. We all three together, here and now, form an alliance that cannot and will not be broken, as the master hood establishes a conduit of the Christ, one person, by one person, by one person. Blessed be. All is forgiven. Thanks be to God!

In His holiness we stand, and together and our holy bond shall never be broken apart; our bond is our light. Delight in it from this day, forever unto eternity, as grace flows where forgiveness goes. Our Holy Mother. Thanks be to God!

In His holiness, I stand before you and Andrea Elizabeth to fortify your main soul's status. See to it that from this day forward you enjoin this great space of your soul; contemplate not if you are worthy, contemplate why you thought you were not. There is never a forsaken soul that isn't worthy of light, and take into great account the fortification of your own deep soul reside, as you sit here and read these words. The work is being done, and overnight you will see that which was once a spectacle of a life is anew, a full-on, grace-filled delight. Live life to the fullest, and always cultivate peace. Be one with the light within, and never go astray again. Long live the queen!

My Day 4 Soul Goal is:
Thought for the day:
Today I wish to live free from ties to my soul, and to live my soul's purpose. May I live this way forevermore.

Chapter 7

Day 5 – Holiness

On this day, Andrea Elizabeth and I set out to fully cultivate and activate a space for holiness. This energetic space plays a part that is only open to me. In the deepness of my own soul journey, I announce the following to the world.

Prayer 8: Daily Togetherness in Partnership Prayer

On this day, I am free of my past endeavors that have caused me un-light. I open up this space, together with the universe at my back, and never again allow non-fortitude to reside in my presence. I am open, free, and grace-filled. I live in the presence of the queen. I am opulent and grand, and forevermore a fortress of light. Amen!

On day 5, let's take a good look at the resonance of our soul's space that has entitled us to be careless in the endeavors of our own selves. Why have we not taken good, or even great, care in our adherence to our wellness? What have we not cared enough about in our own space that we gave up on the lavishness of our soul's character? Where is the love of your character?

Today, let's take a look at which characteristics we have that are so grand, yet we do not allow them to be in the foreground of our world. Let's really dig deep into our soul space and magnify each and every one. These characteristics are the real good in us, the ones that we have pushed to the back of our soul's space. Perhaps deep down you really do love people, yet you keep them at a distance because you were, or are, ashamed, or felt less-than.

Magnifying your soul is what this process is all about; why should everyone else be caring and joyful, while we just sit back and watch? This is our time to perform to the highest standard of our soul's resonance and become fully qualified as a magnificent soul. Sort of like the caterpillar getting its wings, we begin to show and enjoy our own self and our own soul. And in the making, we become fully encapsulated and free.

So now let's list up to 10 things that we keep hidden about ourselves; really examine your own soul space and ask the question "What is it that I love most about myself?"

List the outstanding items:
1)

2)

3)

4)

5)

6)

7)

8)

9)

10)

Then ask yourself, what is hidden deep down within my soul's space that deeply resonates with my goodness? It could be that you love to help little old women across the street. You feel deeply when you see a homeless person. You love animals so much, even more than people that make you cry at their mere presence.

Each of these characteristics has behind it a wellness property, such as compassion, humility, humanity, or love. Behind each and every loving characteristic about yourself is a spiritual principle. So as you list these hidden aspects of you, finding the hidden principle in which you live your life is prevalent or easy to do.

What this exercise is doing is bringing out and allowing you to see that your life is run on deep soul principles that are very different than you thought. Seeing each one on paper really sanctifies the relationship with yourself. And in doing this and having this list in front of you, your eyes are fully open to the resolve that you are truly a well-balanced, light and love of God. You're digging deep into your soul creation space to eliminate any haste, bad or deviant thoughts or feelings about yourself, based upon others' misguided actions, inactions or judgments against you; you are finding out who you are, at your core. And from this space, you will begin to enjoy and love who you really are at this core of your being. Your soul!

Sir Lento has to discuss:

Dearest Andrea,

Bring forth, together with the reader, a grand, reluctant space for doubt. As, even though they make this list, there will be doubt about list, as well. Have the reader create a doubt list on the side, if they must. That way, they are more deeply satisfied with their work. As we all know, no one is perfect. From this doubt list, have them create a new way of thinking about each doubt by listening to their soul's space about each and every doubt. List it, contemplate it, and then ask for any and all forgiveness about this doubt of self. This is a perfectly comparable way of learning how to self-forgive and to self-portray our own real truth of the matter at hand.

Thank you, Master Lento!

My pleasure!

So having read what Sir Lento suggests, let's create a doubt list, contemplate it and then ask for any and all forgiveness about this doubt of self. Allowing Sir Lento and his masters of angels to reside fully in this space of forgiveness, he gives us the following Prayer of Forgiveness:

Prayer 10: Sir Lento Prayer of Forgiveness

On this day, with Sir Lento, the Masters of Angels, Andrea Elizabeth and myself, I further ask for the glory of our creator to fully sanctify my work here today, so that I may fully encapsulate and become present here now, with all the masters of the universe. I currently forgive the following dereliction of my soul in order to become a lover of life, and a giver of light. I ask for pure satisfactory forgiveness for:

1)

2)

3)

4)

5)

6)

7)

8)

9)

10)

As you write each one, give the full explanation of who, what, why, when, and how, and then go on to the next one.

After the list is complete and explanations are written, give it your best blessing with all concerned and move on to the next phase.

All is forgiven here and now, as I live in light with total and complete forgiveness of myself. Forgiveness is my super power.

My Day 5 Soul Goal is:
Thought for the day:
Today I live deeply within the power of forgiveness. May I live this way forevermore.

Chapter 8

Day 6 – The Holy Sacraments With Master Jesus

These Holy Sacraments were derived from a deep resonance within the soul reside. Each and every cataclysmic prophecy rang true at one time. During the great fulfillment space, our encapsulated soul stated the following:

I am, and have forever been, a cataclysmic force of the Gods. Deep within my veins runs the light of the lord, the soul of the heavens. Forgiven not for the lust of the people but for the lust of the light, in each and every capacity I have been given enlightenment. And each and every soul can be given the same.

Write about a time when your soul was at a place where you knew you were doing wrong, and did it anyway. Create a list of at least five decisions and really go deep to the space where the decision was made. And in each creation space or moment of decision, ask for total and complete forgiveness. This cultivates a new beginning of sorts, and really rewrites your history as it should be. We are undoing the past to create a new tomorrow.

Five acts of forgiveness

I ask for total and complete forgiveness for:

1)

2)

3)

4)

5)

Prayer 11: Daily Togetherness in Partnership Prayer
Master Jesus prays with us.
Master Jesus, along with Andrea Elizabeth and I as the writer of this journal, solemnly vow to come together as one to permanently eradicate my past decision-making. In each and every decision, there was a time of judgment. We release this judgment of the action of contrition to become a full-fledged power of the Son. Each time I un-decide my fate, a newness arises in my space and I become whole, little by little, piece by piece. I, who was once fractured, am now an entire section the light.
Blessed be!

My Day 6 Soul Goal is:

Thought for the day:
Today I live deeply within my own power of the Son. May I live this way forevermore.

Chapter 9

Day 7 – Creating Newness With Master Jesus

Corresponding with day six, we now encounter a newness. It could be in the way of delight, joy, sympathy, adherence, or what have you. See how your behaviors are beginning to change as we begin to assist in the changing of the guard, so to speak. As you continually co-create with the Masters and myself, we are creating an alliance that cannot be broken. We are creating a newness space for all new endeavors of your life. We are creating light, or a fortress of light, a place of safety and contentment deep within your soul.

Now, as you go about this next exercise, co-creating with God or the universe, ask yourself, "How does God see me? What are God's thoughts about me, and the past actions of my life?" Now you may say, "I do not know what God thinks," but just act as if you know. Open the bubble, sit and meditate on it, then move forward.

How Does God see Me? What are God's thoughts and ideas about me? Create a list of at least 8 to10 items. For example, you could say:

- God sees me as Goodness. Therefore God sees me as God
- God sees me as Light. Therefore God sees me as enlightened
- God sees me as Drab. Therefore God sees me as blah or unfortunate
- God sees me as Boring. Therefore God sees me as lifeless
- God sees me as Sad. Therefore God sees me as drab
- God sees me as Unethical. Therefore God hates me

Does this make sense? I am having you write your perception of you through God's eyes and feelings. This way, you are able to understand God's feelings about you that are from you. This is really an exercise in cocreating your own light by finding out what sort of discernments you have about how God sees you.

Now begin writing. When you are finished, take a look at each word, and write next to it why you feel this way.

Your perceptions of you:

1)

2)

3)

4)

5)

6)

7)

8)

9)

10)

In all circumstances, you feel this way because you do not acknowledge God's presence in your life or in your space. What we are looking at is how your perception of how God perceives you really creates your reality, and in doing this, you can become further aware of what is happening in your life and in your space. You are cultivating a new, challenging opening for new beginnings in your life.

By using this exercise effectively each day, you will begin to co-manage your life by believing that you and God are one, and that God's presence is with you and in your being space every day. The more you begin this conversation of perception, you will begin ultimately becoming a partner as you will find that God does speak, and God does think, and God even breathes through you—always. This old mismanaged space is going out, and this new partnership is cultivating a new presence in your life. You as God. How magnificent!

Prayer 12: Daily Togetherness in Partnership Prayer

As I sit here together with Andrea Elizabeth and cultivate a newness about me, we are creating a sounding board for the light of God or for the universe to persistently create. We hold tight together within this space of everlasting desire for more light to be given to my opening space and, as the outer armor cracks, the light begins seeping in deeper and deeper and begins to penetrate my old closeted spaces. We are co-creating a new song for my life; we are cultivating light. I now further allow for Andrea Elizabeth to grant the powers of the light to shine in and on my life, and create wellbeing forever more unto eternity. Amen—so be it!

Master Jesus has words:

Dearest friend and Andrea Elizabeth,

Masters are not given, or bought, or made overnight; cultivating lightness takes rough decision-making and hard manifestation work. Dig deeper into your own space so that you may ultimately break through into the walls of desire. The desire for more courage, the desire for more strength, the efficacy of faith, all cultivation of a deeper need for more of the light to shine in. For future endeavors, always encompass your strengths first, as then your weaknesses will diminish in their light; search far and wide for answers, as the more you see, the further you come to find your ownership in light.

Blessed be!

Thank you, Master Jesus!

Master Jesus:

Answers come to all who seek. Blessed be the ones to whom the light is their pathway.

My Day 7 Soul Goal is:

Thought for the day:

Today I live deeply in the desire for more light through courage. May I live this way forevermore.

Chapter 10

Day 8 – The Universal Mind With Pythagoras

On this gracious day, together we are cultivating a more strict adherence to our own grounded de-light space in this universal mind. In this universal mind, we solemnly find that if we are together in one mind, in one sound, in one song or resonance, we are all the same together, as one grand manifestation. On this 8th day of contrition, we formally contemplate our old song. What did we used to sound like? What did we formerly vibrate? How did our old song co-create our lives with ourselves and others?

Pythagoras has words on this:

Good morning, Andrea Elizabeth, and to our newest friend here. I hope and wish in this admonishment of your own vibration, you can begin to cultivate a newness in your biological systemic makeup. Together with all the angels, guides, masters, ascended masters, and past mythological beings, we can co-create together a newness of sound sincerely particular to you. Here now. We articulate to you the following design for mastery of your own sound. First, find a particular resonance that sounds or seems off to you. It could be a particular person, it could be a particular feeling, or a particular thought about something that really makes you irritated. Now think about this. After you find the first one that comes to mind, really look at this thing, or person, or place that keeps you off-balance. Now, when you are off-balance, you are out of tune musically. In the Universe you have your own specific resonating vibration that interludes between the heavens and creates a sort of divine liturgy, so to speak. You create your own heaven, of sorts. And when your magic is off-resonance, the universal mind becomes off a bit. Do you follow me?

If each person on earth is out of balance significantly and harmonically, then the entire Universe becomes a latent tune of almost-discord and then your body frequency becomes off, your mind becomes off, and your soul becomes off. So as you look at this particular item that has you off-balance, really see it for what it is. Really take a good look musically at its proportion of light. How much of your light does this particular item take up of you today? And if you were to be rid of it, how much more light could you carry?

For this next exercise, in accordance within the area of sound, write down at least 8 items that create discord in your life today.

1)

2)

3)

4)

5)

6)

7)

8)

We are working here in the present. Really see the dis-value in your life. Then determine how many actually don't exist, then delete them, then find the ONE that stands out the most. When this is complete, see this idea, or scene, or person, place, or thing in your mind's eye. And just OM it out from your heart center.

Using this OM exercise allows for you to clear out your realm of self allowing in other possibilities. Going back to the list, OM out each and every one of these items that create a dissatisfied feeling in your space. Really feel from your heart center as you OM these particular items out of your space. When you have OM'd the entire list out of your space, give one great big OM, and feel the difference in your space.

You will feel much more clear, and vibratory, and in sync with your soul.

Prayer 13: Daily Togetherness in Partnership Prayer

Prayer from the Greeks: Pythagoras, along with Andrea Elizabeth and our new friend. On this spectacular day of OM, we bring in the alliance of the creator. As a spark of the divine enters our friend's heart and the oldness slips away, may their heart, soul and vibration be renewed to a level of deep understanding, truth and co-existence with all that is. There is a frequency we all allow, and now it resides deep within our new friend.

Blessed be, and glory be to God!

May all your future endeavors carry the greatest of frequencies deep within your soul resonance, so that you may touch the souls of the Son. Peace be to God!

My Day 8 Soul Goal is:

Thought for the day:

Today I deeply resonate within the Universal OM. I am the Universal OM. May I live this way forevermore.

Chapter 11
DAY 9 – FINDING YOUR MAGNIFICENCE WITH PYTHAGORAS

In literal terms, we all sort of side-step our own magnificence. Yet we all wish for miracles. In this next piece, we ultimately return to the divine within so that we may coexist or coincide shortly, close to a miracle. Each and every miracle blessing has its own resonance, and its own formidable gain of accessing our own deep truth within. The reside within us has such a powerful magnificence that there sometimes comes a need to show it.

In this next section, we will begin showing our own true self from deep within the reside of our soul, and we will uncover our own greatest hidden things, or assets. From this space, we will accentuate our own privity, and we will begin to coexist with what is inside us to formulate a true, concrete relationship with our soul at a level never before known. This solstice is the emergence of our own truest being, or our true self, at a level never before or even rarely seen. To activate our space, let us all pray the following statement.

Prayer 14

I, along with Andrea Elizabeth, Pythagoras and all the Greek Gods of our time, staggeringly open our illicit soul space and create a working space of heaven. Here, we essentially reunify the old with the new.

We open our soul as much as we can, and begin to rely upon our faith from above, as well as our own soul space. We today will begin to co-inspire, co-create, and co-manufacture all that has been lacking here deep within your reside. We fully activate the soul resonance from the singing of the heavenly spheres and covertly uncover my song of my truth.

My Song of My Truth

My soul cries out for the Gods above, and they have come forth and answered. You are the truest of true lights, all within the deepest part of heaven above. You truly resound light, love, and a sort of covert loveliness that you wish few to see. We come here to open this loveliness now and forevermore, so that you shall be able to sing your song openly, excitedly, and wondrously. Here is your song.

Now begin to sit in this loving space with these Gods, in their energy, and write Your Song. Do so lovingly, in a kind, thoughtful manner, and interpret the song of your soul.

The song of my soul begins with:
I belong deeply to the center of my soul existence. I sing from the depths of my valleys within. I cultivate light from these valleys by reminiscing and inspiring the light within to become _____

_____

_____

_____

After you have finished, put this away for a day, then read it again. You will be in total and complete joy at the outcome.

Prayer 14: Prayer With the Angels for the Closing of Your Song of Your Soul

I ask now in the presence of the most high, that I sing this song within the heavens for the rest of my life and into eternity. May I be permitted to shine like the wildflowers deep under the summer sky of sheer harmony and delight. I ask for the divine within to come forth, and I will live as though there is nothing blocking my path, as I am divine, I am the soul of the creator, now and forevermore. Blessed be. Thanks be to God. The angels have spoken. May the divine light reside so deeply within that there shall be no further doubt of the light.

My Day 9 Soul Goal is:

Thought for the day:

Today I sing the song of my soul, loud, and proud. May I live this way forevermore.

Chapter 12

DAY 10 – CREATING VOWS OF MY SOUL WITH MOSES

Today as we take a look back at your Soul Song, let us begin to resonate in your space with the utmost loveliness of the heavens. Allowing in the multiplicity of the angel realms, the heavenly spheres of song as well, and the full-on Christed Beings of all times.

As you read this, begin to allow a magnanimous crystal-clear white-light energy to flow down from the heavenly spheres and into the crown of your head. Allow the flow of this white light in and through your entire body, and down through your feet into the earth mother.

Sit with this for a bit, as you begin to feel the flow of the heavenly realm. Be present, in this day, in this time, here now, sit and allow this heavenly flow to begin an infiltration of your remaining space of light. Allow the various heavenly realms to bequeath to you a song of delight, a song of harmony, a song of wellness, and a song of truth. Your truth.

For those spaces of self that you still wish to hold onto, allow for the heavenly realm to infiltrate each and every aspect of you that still has doubts that you are the chosen one, that you are enlightened, that you actually have a Soul Song. Just let these doubts be softly taken over with the love that is here now, and let it flow deeply into each crevice of your soul. Sit with this for awhile.

Co-creating with the masters is a mindset. We must believe so that we can. This is what Moses always says to me. Moses has words for today:

Greetings, Andrea Elizabeth and our new friend of the light. In absolute grand thought, in absolute grand magnificence, and in an absolute grand epiphany, allow in the elusive tranquility that so many seek. Yes, we all seek to have solace and quiet time, but what about the tranquility of the elusive soul that keeps us hidden, year after year, and time after time? Does anyone really pray to seek that? I bring in this tranquility for our new friend to write a new vow for themself on this day. It can be a vow of living, it can be a vow of loving, and it can even be a vow of disillusionment, meaning that even if one does not believe these writings, they can write it anyway.

In this vow we wish for you to include a harmonious remnant of the deepest of the deep burrows of your soul, a vow to which you can supersede all other vows.

This will be a contrition vow for your own life. It will become your new song, to include your newfound music and fruition-based light. It will be as if you have switched out of the old and realigned a new you. Go ahead and try it!

- I vow to become a supplicant, filled with grace and grandeur forever more.
- I vow to allow only light into my life. (There could be two vows.)
- I vow for only freedom to be my vow for my life. (There could be three vows.)

We are vowing here in almost an adolescent space so that we can rewrite our light or life. These vows, or affirmations, will become our new journey; to accentuate our space, so that the old can be removed and the new can come in.

When finished with your vows, write each of them on a card or paper, and then each day pick up a new vow to state for the day. A sort of vow-a-day card.

Each day pick one card and repeat it as many times as possible. You can say it out loud, you can sing it while driving in the car, and you can write it and really begin to believe it. Doing this exercise changes our thoughts about any specific ideas and allows change to happen.

You can write the vows on 3x5" cards or sticky notes and put them on mirrors, or you can even journal new vows each day. Write them on sticky notes and put them all over your house. Always do this with the strict intention of lighting your soul on fire and changing your soul's resonance so that you can become free from the past.

Prayer 15: Closing Prayer

From this day forward, I, along with Andrea Elizabeth, Moses, and his disciples, formally grant that I shall be renewed with a new sense of delight and grand fortitude. I shall prevail in absolutely everything I set out to accomplish in grace, and love.

So be it!

My Day 10 Soul Goal is:

Thought for the day:

I live my vows of change today. May I live this way forevermore.

Chapter 13

Day 11 – Finding Grace Within With Our Blessed Mother

Finding grace is such a grand endeavor, yet it is, and has always been, right here in front of us. Grace was never lost or far from us; we just had not been able to see it. Once we become in alignment with that vibration of grace, the world simply seems to conspire to assist us in our grandeur of simplicity and delight.

To begin, we must be or become a symbol of the grandness of the light, which to me is simply grace, a God-given right of design from the wisdom of the universe, maybe even from the heavens, or from the Gods. Grace originated somewhere deep within the conjecture of God; somewhere in man and somewhere in our soul and its creations are also the sun and the moon. At the very time of our creation, there was a sudden spark, a sound, a light, a resonance and boom! Our grace was born as we were born. Yet, somewhere, some of us have forgotten that we are born of grace, we are born of love, and we are born of forgiveness. We slather on the protective armor or build a wall sometimes so as to not be able to vibrate the resonance of grace, because we feel at times we are so unworthy.

Mother Mary speaks:

Greetings, beloved one, and Andrea Elizabeth, you are beloved too. I am here to tell you a story of one who had great issues with feeling that she was privy to any grace in her life. Her name is Andrea Elizabeth. For approximately 3 years, Andrea Elizabeth's Angels, Master Jesus, and I would channel ideas and words, information, writings, and prayers to her. She would hear us, stop and begin to cry, because in her heart she could not fathom the fact that the heavens were trying to speak to her. She had great problems with herself, and her life, and her love for herself.

However, little by little, we taught her about love, about faith, about grace, and how allowing these in her life made changes in the facets of her intelligence, her strife, and her couth. She felt as though she was not allowed to hear us and would cry because she felt so unworthy. So we worked with her, and each time she would cry, we would allow her, her tears, and when they would stop she would say, "Why me?" and we would ask, "Why not you? Why are you not worthy of Christ? You have done the work."

And her mind would wander to the other people she thought she should be working with, as she felt as though what she was receiving was only for others, and she did not deserve to have such special attention. We would stop her and say, "Andrea Elizabeth, you have done this work for so many years and have become a clear, effervescent conduit of the Creator. Who are you to say you are not worthy?"

And each time we would stop her and say this, she would allow us to continue. It took some time for us to convince her, but one day she finally caught herself welling-up with tears. Finally, her own mind said, "You are worthy!" And at that moment, she felt that she could do this work, and had the ability or worthiness to hear us.

The point being here that Andrea Elizabeth was able to begin to change her thoughts about herself, and that is when the true grace of a loving Creator began pour come in.

Thank you, Blessed Mother!

My pleasure!

Side note: As I was editing this, I broke down and cried like never before. I almost felt like the story of Jesus on the cross, dying for the truth of our souls. I began to allow in all the grace, and all of the love of God, and all of the magnificence that has been waiting so long for me to allow in. I have to admit, it was very painful having to allow in with such wonder and succession. Maybe the prayer I jotted down will give more clarity.

Prayer 16: Flourish by Allowing Grace

I allow, for I am not forsaken. I am alive with full vigor and grace, for it is by my own true will of God that I flourish. Blessed be.

I now add this Grace Box Exercise given to me by my guides.

Opening Your Grace Box

In this Opening of your Grace Box exercise, together we will work through and find all things that have been undoing minimal amounts of grace during the course of your life. This undoing of grace has its own way of disavowing itself from you, allowing bits of grace to creep in at times, but mostly keeping grace out. Our thoughts, deeds, and feelings create a bubble of unwellness or disgrace around us, and we allow what is in this bubble to decide what is right for us, even if we think we were right in many of our decisions in our life.

If you really think about it, our past thoughts actually do create our reality. If you are in a doubting space or self-despising space, or if unloved aspects of you are ruling, running, and co-creating your world, you will only achieve mildly attributed grace.

However, if you are creating from a totally clean slate of grace in your world, you will be able to allow in the grace and attribute that grace to your own handsome space of a true master. Mastering grace is difficult in our society, because we always think that we are lacking something. Something others flash in front of us, or we see on media that says we must have THIS thing, or THAT thing to be happy. However, our happiness actually stems from our own being. Our own thoughts, feelings, deeds, emotions, and accepted grace. Let's say a prayer together for the following work so that it becomes easier for you to proceed.

Prayer 17: Prayer of Essential Grace
As we open this bubble of essential grace, we ask this day that I be allowed to fortify my life by knowing that there is true grace available to me. I now attempt to live in a state of grace, allowing in the good and the light for once and for all. I am filled with the spirit of grace as I do the following exercise:
Blessed be!

Let us begin with you taking a look at yourself from the outside in. See yourself with your "inside eyes," notice your space as though you're looking out the window of your soul space, take a right step out of your body and turn around and look at yourself. Now can you see yourself, or allow yourself to get in touch with this space of yourself? Just sit and allow it to become a mirror image of yourself, as though you are sitting in front of yourself, viewing yourself. Now, if you have difficulty using your mind's eye, sit in front of a mirror and try the following:

Your Mind's Eye

As you see yourself spiritually, what do you notice? Do you notice any boxes or blocks? These blockages are your life's grace hindrances. They may show up as circles, dark masses, bubbles, faces, pictures, ideas, even memories—anything in your space that looks like a blockage to you.

These blocks will show up in a form that only you can understand, because this is you speaking to yourself on a higher level of understanding.

This is a sort of self-communication, and the more you get to know yourself, the more you will understand how you speak to yourself

For this exercise, I suggest you get quiet and put in your earplugs for a couple minutes. When you feel you have seen your blockages, begin writing them down.

Blockages – What Is The Cause of This Block

_____
_____
_____
_____
_____
_____

As you write each block, what are the feelings you get associated with it? As you get each particular feeling, ask:

- Why do I have these feelings?
- Why do I have this block? Why is this feeling associated with it?

Go back in over and over and keep asking why. Each blockage, go deeper, and deeper, and deeper. We are going to get to the crux of your un-grace.

Blocks could be:
- Where I lived.
- How my parents acted, if they fought or didn't fight. If there was no conflict growing up, what led to you not learning how to handle conflicts in relationships?
- How I was treated as a child by the neighborhood kids.
- How I felt I denied myself happiness, based on any of these questions.
- How I felt I should suffer for my parents' behaviors.

Anything that comes to your mind. Stay here and allow the feelings and emotions you have with each one, and the reasoning behind them.

Really sit with each one, and create notes behind the blocks.

When you feel you have found all the blocks that are cutting you off from your deservance of grace, allow each blockage to slowly fall off, one by one. As you acknowledge each one, notice the block, then just allow it to fall off. Look at each one without thinking about it any longer, or judging it, and continue writing for as long as you like.

Then, when you feel completely cleansed of each blockage and feeling behind it, look up and see the essence of grace coming down through your crown and into your entire body space.

Simply and slowly allow this essence to dance in and though your space, filling up the broken parts of you and your empty spaces of all this self-denial of grace.

As you sit with this grace energy flow, see it as a golden molasses flow of grace. Allow this grace to overcome your space, feel it permeate and flow entirely over your body space, and begin to expel all negativity from your space over your entire timeline. Feel the molasses blend covering your entire body and permeating all your space with grace, really allowing it in and letting it begin to fortify your space with its presence.

Prayer 18: Allowance of Grace

Say to yourself this prayer of allowing grace into your life:

As I allow this flow of grace into my life, I allow it to wash away all characteristics of my past, and I allow myself to be grace and to live within my space of greatness with the allowance of grace all of the time. Blessed be!

Sit with this prayer for a bit, allowing the full essence of this grace prayer to resonate and commingle within your new beautiful healing space of grace and forgiveness. Sit here until you are ready to begin affirming grace.

Allow this energy flow to take away all bad thoughts of your timelines and your past lives. This exercise will help alleviate all the unseen bad or unacceptable difficulties that happened as a result of your negative thoughts and feelings.

Sit with this for a bit, allow the grace energy to have a color, if you like, and continue to see it from outside yourself, cleaning and cleansing and opening up your soul to goodness. As you see this cleaning and cleansing happening to you, also feel it flowing down into your space of wellness.

Mother Mary adds:
Give yourself this gift of grace today. By allowing grace in, you move away from sadness; by allowing grace in, you allow hatred out; by allowing grace to flow within your space, all other deviations no longer persist. You no longer have to be what others thought you had to be; you can now just be grace. And as you are grace, feel the vibration of love and kindness; feel this gratitude for yourself; keep your eyes turned inward for now, and just feel your love for yourself, your grace, and your gratitude for the gifts you have here on earth at this time. Take a good look at your love and your wellness space within. It is growing and flowing with grace.

With your hands on your heart space, sit with these feelings a bit, and watch grace flow and permeate all that you are—inside and out.

As this flows, allow the old you to disappear into the earth and be regenerated by the grace of our Mother.

Mother earth is happy to take our old stuff; she regenerates it into a golden love for the masses, so never feel bad for allowing your negativity to fall off. It's the cycle of life, really.

One never has enough life cycles to un-deny this, as our love for mother earth is renowned and indescribable. Its feelings are a source of very dominant trust and delight. We were each created with this, so let's return to that space or source of love, delight, and trust, first for our self, then for our mother earth, then for the universe.

This trifecta allows us the power and the resonance to become far less divisive by our generation, as well as our surroundings. Be the light within, so that others may smile and acknowledge their own space of grace and light within.

This will undeniably revolutionize our canonization process, as one God is our God. All religions are hoping to find out what their God is and can do; however, they miss the mark every time, as one God is our God, the all-powerful, the all-knowing, the God of Gods. He who has God has grace. Period. There is nothing left to say; God is not out there, God is inside. As each person has his own awakening of a loving personal God, nothing else will matter. All deficits will be regained, and we will become whole again. There will be no feelings of lack or lust; the love of the truth will suffice.

Everything will be revealed and healed to be lived. There will be no more loneliness or spite. One must give of oneself. So to die in order to live, one must un-create in order to co-create.

So that we are one with the Master, we must undo our past thoughts, actions, and deeds about and within ourselves, to become new and whole—the way we were meant to live, as a living, breathing God.

Creating Grace Affirmations

Finally, let us create some Grace Affirmations to coincide with our work on this day. The more we acknowledge our grace from within, the more we will acknowledge our grace from without. Creating cards, or notes, or reminders on a daily basis keeps us in the strategy of living grace and continually adding to our Grace Box.

Some good affirmations could be:
- Grace flows within me
- I am grace
- I allow grace
- Grace is life
- Simply grace
- I am filled with Grace

Any and all affirmations are incredibly helpful, and either creating new affirmations or picking a new card each day and putting it where we can see it, or taping it on our mirror in the bathroom, or putting in on the dashboard in our car, the more we see the reminders, the more we will be reminded or our grace. This is such a simple, yet effective, exercise in knowing all aspects of our own grace within.

My Day 11 Soul Goal is:
Thought for the day:
Today, I allow the flow of grace. May I live this way forevermore.

Chapter 14

Day 12 – The Unseen Forces Within With Our Blessed Mother and the Heavenly Angels

On this day, we co-create a promise to our soul that from each and every day forward, the answers that lie within come fruitfully and magically to the center of our being, so that our cache may open and be discovered in order for us to rise and become bliss. Each and every soul life has a deep magic within; however, it is rarely seen. On this particular day, we adhere to the particular space that has gone untouched within. Your own personal "Deep Space Nine." A place of promise, of light, and of the Imaginary Muse. Your old or elder soul-self can and will conspire with this, as we have by now taken off a few layers of the old you. Let's say a prayer of truth for our soul.

Chapter 14

DAY 12 – THE UNSEEN FORCES WITHIN WITH OUR BLESSED MOTHER AND THE HEAVENLY ANGELS

On this day, we co-create a promise to our soul that from each and every day forward, the answers that lie within come fruitfully and magically to the center of our being, so that our cache may open and be discovered in order for us to rise and become bliss. Each and every soul life has a deep magic within; however, it is rarely seen. On this particular day, we adhere to the particular space that has gone untouched within. Your own personal "Deep Space Nine." A place of promise, of light, and of the Imaginary Muse. Your old or elder soul-self can and will conspire with this, as we have by now taken off a few layers of the old you. Let's say a prayer of truth for our soul.

within ourselves, to become new and whole—the way we were meant to live, as a living, breathing God.

Creating Grace Affirmations

Finally, let us create some Grace Affirmations to coincide with our work on this day. The more we acknowledge our grace from within, the more we will acknowledge our grace from without. Creating cards, or notes, or reminders on a daily basis keeps us in the strategy of living grace and continually adding to our Grace Box.

Some good affirmations could be:
- Grace flows within me
- I am grace
- I allow grace
- Grace is life
- Simply grace
- I am filled with Grace

Any and all affirmations are incredibly helpful, and either creating new affirmations or picking a new card each day and putting it where we can see it, or taping it on our mirror in the bathroom, or putting in on the dashboard in our car, the more we see the reminders, the more we will be reminded or our grace. This is such a simple, yet effective, exercise in knowing all aspects of our own grace within.

My Day 11 Soul Goal is:

Thought for the day:

Today, I allow the flow of grace. May I live this way forevermore.

Mother Mary would like to be a part of this prayer, as she also brings in her band of singing angels this day.

Prayer 19:

Heavenly Father, on this day, please allow our new friend to become an open vessel for the changes that are about to take place within. Allow for a grand entrance of the coming of the real truth that resides within. In allowance with all main aspects of their health, wealth, and courage, allow all the happiness, and joy, and gratitude to come forward in such a way that has never been seen prior to this day. In the greatness of the masses of the band of the angelic realm, I bring in this day forevermore that the truth be bestowed for laughter, grace, and the grandest fortitude of and for the Christ.

Blessed be our Lord. Blessed Be.

Thank you, Blessed Mother!

My pleasure. May all true beings be enlightened on this very day of truth. God bless!

So now, as our beloved mother departs, allow in any and all aspects of your own inner soul truth to step forward and to realign with you and our entire glorious space. Now step forward and feel the gravity of this magnificent light. Sit in it, laugh in it, run in it, and be in it, always. What is to be accomplished here is for your own beauty, grace, and truth to be reestablished as you become one with you and our truth.

So if you are faltering on your truth, let's define it for you.

Truth can be explained as simply as, I am a soul. There is truth to that, yes? Or, I am derived from the heavens—now there can be some truth to that.

But what exactly is your truth? What inside of you holds the key to your success? It is indelibly your own truth. And once you know your own truth, your heaven inside cannot be denied. It is that simple; know thyself. This has been written over, and over again. Know thyself, and in so doing, you shall know thy soul. And this is where you wish to be, and live from your soul. Period. Nothing else. So by now, on this 12th day, you have been able to co-create yourself from an almost clean slate. Let's finish the job at truth.

Ask yourself, as a spiritual being in a human body, what is the utmost truth about me? How can I portray the highest version of who I am?

Together with Mother Mary, all of our angels, and guides, let's open up a bubble of truth to work in. As we open up a bubble, let's state the following admonition: I, along with the blessed mother, her band of angels, and Andrea Elizabeth, open up a huge bubble of light in which to begin working so that I may further enhance my light. In this bubble, I will openly, discreetly, and honestly bring forth my unopened truths about myself. They could be hidden magic, human mistakes that I have the ability to know things that are going to happen in the future. As of right now, we do not know, but we are all here willing to hold the energy of the light in this bubble and allow the work to come into being.

So be it!

Now begin to ask from the inside. "What are the unopened truths about my soul?"

Examples:
- An unopened truth about me is: That I resonate the presence of God on a daily basis.
- An unopened truth about me is: That my soul resides on a different plane than the earth.
- An unopened truth about me is: That my soul reads other souls.
- An unopened truth about me is: That my soul talks to animals.

Whatever comes up first jot it down, as these are the real unopened truths that deeply penetrate your living space. Stay deep within the resonances of your soul space—not your head, not your heart, but your soul. It resides deeply in the center of your core, just in back of your heart and 3rd chakra; in that space, there is a deep crevice that houses your soul. Ask to speak from that area, not from your heart or your head. Let's begin with your hands on your upper belly area, where your soul resides.

Answer the following:

The unopened truth of my soul is that _____

_____

The unopened truth of my soul is that _____
_____

The unopened truth of my soul is that _____
_____

Begin with a few unopened truths, then really go deep. The deeper you go, the more soul knowledge comes up to the surface. As you look at what you wrote, what jumps out? Go to that sentence and ask again; what do I use this tool for in my life? Ask again and then begin writing.

Next, go down each list and ask the same question: What do I use this tool for in my life? And this is how you find your magical gifts, or tools. Use this as an exercise often when you become stuck in your own head or heart. Always ask from your soul space; that's the real unopened or newly realized truth about who you are.

Create a list of soul unopened or newly realized truths to come back to later, and remember, I am this or that; I forgot. Create cards or letters or stickers or even symbols to remind you of each new realized truth. And by remembering these new truths all the time and seeing them working in your life all around, they will eventually be a natural part of you, both on the inside and outside. Once these unopened truths have been acknowledged and then realized, they will begin to appear in your life. This is key.

My Day 12 Soul Goal is:

Thought for the day:

Today I know myself deeply. May I live this way forevermore.

Chapter 15

Day 13 – Commingling Assets With Master Jesus

Commingling assets: what does this entail? Well, first, as we have seen, we have gifts and assets within ourselves that we had not known about 12 days ago. Who knew? Well, God knew. And as I sat down to write this book in Australia, I honestly had no idea what was to be coming through. This is such an honorable and noble gift. A gift to literally begin to help to assist and to bring out the goodness in others. I honestly have no words, just sheer excitement. So thank you all for reading this. As I write this part for Day 13, Master Jesus would like to explain comingling assets.

Good morning, Master Jesus!

Greetings from the Lord above to my friend Andrea Elizabeth, and to whosoever is at this moment reading this loving book.

As we all have our own past, we all also have our own future. It summons ways of delight and insurmountable assets, such as the health of the land of promise. And there, we are given the gift of humility, and once again we become humbled at the fact that every day, we are given the gift of life. We did not die the day before, nor did we die in our sleep. So we are far more grateful to be alive, and in love, and in joy with our own humanness, and therefore in love with life. As we counteract our souls on a daily basis—commingling our assets of the past with the assets of the future or the day—we happily give source to our lives by becoming a servant to our maker in ways we would never begin to imagine. For instance, has anyone ever thought of the time when they were, say, pushed over a cliff, only to find that the cliff was very close to the ground. And in that time, what was the greatest asset that came to your mind? Grace, or gratitude, or hate, or discouragement? Probably all of them. At first you probably felt discouragement or even hate at being pushed over, and then gratitude that the ground was close. I use this animation and its simplicity for three reasons; One, we have daily ups and downs with our emotions and their plentitude of non-grace; two, we sometimes fully capitulate them; and three, sometimes we even lack the ability to see the God, or soul, or even humanity in others, as we are so encapsulated by our own life. Stuck in such a place of honor vs. dishonor, love vs. hate, good vs. evil, we are in a constant battle within our own embodiment of our life. A mere shell of existence.

So here I behold to you the uncouthness or unfamiliarity of forever, inasmuch as I bring forth a new tomorrow for your perusal. A tomorrow of, say, "commingled assets." All gifts from tomorrow are gifts of today, which are also gifts from yesterday, and so on. This means that each and every moment of our life becomes a gift.

As soon as we see the current moment as bliss or blissful, if we live in the here and now blissfully in each and every breath, we become a literal anomaly of the Christ—meaning we have overcome all commingled assets without having to do or be any of these, we just are. We become healed from our past, we become freed from our prisons, as all of these are simply a farce. Keep out the goings-on with the former or the latter, and sorely become hateful, or even have distaste for heaven. This distaste seemingly goes away with the pretense that we never really were, or we never really are. We cannot be in the present moment, because there are so many things to accomplish, and accomplishments are a huge duty for the masses. You do not have to be that way; you can simply be, and have bliss. You choose! I have mastered this in such a way that I entrain my own thoughts to simply be, and I am in alignment with the masses on a level yet unheard of. Their own bliss is spotty, at best, yet I know there is bliss in each person, and I can sometimes co-exist with some of them; others, not so much.

So, for the most part, few find this space of bliss, and few live in and from it. We have a literal choice: to be, or not to be. So as we keep our mind focused here now and with a spectacular view of our soul, we begin to intertwine our heart with our soul and with our mind. We can literally do this by simply being here, now, and forevermore one with the Creator. So I give to you a vibratory resonance to practice so that you may find peace.

The Seven Sounds of Love (Indian Sanskrit Tantric Sounds)

SA (Root)
RE (Pelvis)
GA (Solar plexus)
MA (Heart)
PA (Throat)
DHA (3rd eye)
NI (Back of head)
SA (Crown)

This is the vibratory resonance for the NOW. Use this often to stay focused in the here and now, and to beguile or charm your soul.

Godspeed to all to read this!

Thank you so much, Master Jesus!

My pleasure. Thanks be to God!

What this exercise will give you is the resonance of becoming blissful, free, and yielding a new sense of light. Do this exercise every day until you finish this book, then remember to regain this temperament every time you are off balance. This sort of healing vibration or resonance regains your space, or your diffident soul. It co-regulates your adaptive living space, or life space, here on earth, and allows the seminal space to regain further recognition for your life. You are bliss, and are blissfully loved forevermore.

My Day 13 Soul Goal is:

Thought for the day:

Today I live deeply within my reside of bliss. May I live this way forevermore.

Chapter 16
Day 14 – Relevant to God With Einstein and Sir Isaac Newton

So by now there should be some massive changes in your space. Do you feel normal, sad, mad, glad, or indifferent? How is your magical glow? Has anyone noticed a difference? Have you noticed a difference? Inside? Outside? All over?

Now, as we begin to regulate daily a new way of adjusting to living from the inside, we somehow seem to deviate a bit from the norm. If you feel a bit off, go back through your daily writings and find where you have misplaced you. It should be very easy by now. Also, you may call upon all of us to help in your reside. Remember, each day we open up a bubble of strength, courage, aptitude, and grace. It never, ever goes away. It is open and has tremendous staying power. Be there in that bubble and find the parts of you that you lost.

So here we are at 14 days, 2 parts of 7 each. This brings in our old friend Albert Einstein, who pops his brilliant head in once in a while. How do I know this? Well, to begin with, he always has some sort of a derivative of a math solution. Usually he brings in Sir Isaac Newton to pick my brain, as well. So let's see who shows up.

Greetings to you, Albert Einstein and Sir Isaac! What say you?

Sir Isaac says "Marvelous, my dear, Marvelous."

Thank you both for being here and bringing part of you magic to this book.

We are here to simply cater to your own working, or ways, of how you actually use the multiplication or the physics of light. Your own organization of time co-creates a distant reality where one can actually behave differently, even if he does not see the need to. You are organizing a sort of multiplicity realm for those who are already noticing differences, and have a keen sense of time, or of the timeline diversion.

So first, the explanation: We, Sir Isaac and I, find it an indelible feat that one must have to read books in order to find one's soul. In our time, it seems we were more privy to Christ, or the Christ of our own inner being. This is only because we scientists or physicists can't believe in religion, as it is not a well-thought-out process, and we found it uncanny that all the followers were like sheep being led to slaughter.

We also found that the universe, or universal conjecture, or relevant misgivings, we had about God were as absurd as the leaves of a tree not changing colors in the fall. As before, most of us were unmuted and able to forgive the unforgiven or the, say, unrelatable or unknowledgeable. The universe is as vast as our mind can imagine. So we began to ponder. Say, for instance, how can one say that our moon only stays to the right, as we see it formulate to the left, etc.? It moves, right? Yes. Well then our idea of catharsis is one of ideally persnickety, as one may think that one's idea is the only right one. And should it be known that there is more than one idea, then it shall be looked at. Insomuch as our own validation of truth comes from a deep crevice within our soul being.

And to gather more information on this is rather indelible as truth in our manner of living.

If you give someone a book to study, and he looks at the only basic text and not the illume, he misses the entire premise of the book.

If we look only solely at our body as a masterpiece of heaven, yet explore not our inside, then we are not fully examining our truth. What is the antithesis of our own soul? In retrospect, it is heaven. We are heaven, we hold a heavenly presence deep within.

What we are bringing here this day for your writings, Andrea Elizabeth, is to give to you the furtherance of a depiction of time. As time flows back and forth into future reality, it also moves back and forth widely to overcome the most unnatural forms of dissociation of, or in the timeline of, heavenly space, or its own, or one's depiction of time, or their current timeline on earth.

In heaven, we rely solely on a magnanimous effort as an unusual space for what you all depict as time. We in heaven all depict this as relevance. As relevance creates harmonious laughter among the triads. In the smashing of the universal timeline, relevance is divided by numerous dividers, to which all fall aback to the past.

The bridled forces of, say, a tourniquet are sometimes the living apathy of the survival, say, of the unhinged arm. So to cut off one's arm to save ones, say, stalemate is not a beginning of sorts; it is a legacy to become unearthed fully and opulently. We devise a space here and now to become to emulate a, or the, or its, vast, say, tourniquet of God. As once it was cut off or shut off, once it began to stay motivated to be something other than itself.

When one is itself, negated, it defies or denies itself and then furthermore remains hidden. However, when one nullifies the present, or, say, a past remedy for what seemingly ails you, one becomes a sort of defiant illusion. We begin to live an illusory acquaintance with God, and with a future between the lines of deception. So we reiterate this with a sound mind-body notion. He that doth the latter will

unjunctify one's past to be in the present.
Basically stating that y-a=b.
Y is the future.
A is the past.
B is the present.

Unify your biased opinion as the Holy Christed Being to become an unsaturated, limitless, divine creator of and for the masses. Our service to the world is our very capable light. We all will seem to endeavor the most untrustworthy of things and seemingly become frail; however, each step we take toward municiplicity or one's, say, torque gives of great value to those here on earth. Otherwise, we nullify our being.

If we do not use our gifts to assist humanity, we forgo our magnificence and become smaller, little by little by little. And that is no way to live.
Thank you, Einstein and Sir Isaac!

Our very pleasure my dear. We both raise hope that the reader operates under the guise of I in thee, and thee in thou, as here we proceed with Nostradamus to explain further.
Greetings, Nostradamus!
Greetings, dear Andrea Elizabeth, and to the new choice of reader, welcome!

A great story of Nostradamus and his grand degree of sight

Here is Nostradamus who had great success with the wealth of humanity. He seemingly lived on borrowed time, as he very well knew when he would submit to Christ. And at some point he relayed information about the destruction of the Twin Towers in New York, the Enron breakdown, and many other diverse goings on here on our planet in present time.

He yielded, however, to the fact that when he spoke, ordinary people took notice because of his ownership of his guise. He knew he was full of truth and knowledge, and therefore he knew God not literally, but unilaterally and faithfully. All his gathered information came from the Holy Christed Being deep within, and he masterfully found a faith that mattered to him.

Unbeknownst to all others and all other facets of his time period or realms of his lifetime, he gave all to be all. All so that many others may be found. Meaning that he lived his truth as an honorary badge of light. He gave so that others may live. He shared his profoundness with the world in order to bring light to a seemingly dim existence. He shared his utmost truth of God or himself in order for others to be privy to their own truth. He did not share his advancement of his own knowingness just for excitement or vengeance, he did it so that others, too, may find the God within and form a union so as to bequeath Christ at a level of disparity and lavishness. He gave so that others may live. But so many others took not the Christ light and endeavored a limited life of unworthiness.

In summation, it seems that these writings, along with Andrea Elizabeth, are being foretold deeply and magnificently and are developmentally sound. She has the gift and the wealth of sight. So what we bring today is for you to break your illusion of your own sight. Imagine if you could know things so deeply inside that you needed no other authentication or identification. If you knew who you were deep inside, at your core, would you seek outside otherwise?

Today we ask that you take a moment and shield yourself with a space of relevance. How am I relevant to me? How am I relevant to God? What do I do with this relevance? Do I accomplish my life's goal with it? Some deep questions, we are sure, with some even deeper answers. Rely solely here, as you write in your soul base. Begin from that deep space within to really begin to verify your relevance. At the beginning, it may be tough. But really sit with this for a bit. The answers will come when you are ready. And by now, in reading in this book of crazed healing days, sorry Andrea. It is a lot. We see exactly where and why she has written this. As we did our best to formulate some type of wealth within during our lifetimes.

Andrea Elizabeth has found the magical key, and wishes for you to have it as well. The hidden mastery key is you, inside. There is no denying this, as you look back at the day's writings and see your own magnificence. It is true, and it is on paper now. This way, you may begin to eliminate all in your life that

isn't true and is counter-effective or counter-efficient to you living free from your past self and beginning to shine as a true magnificence of your soul space deep inside. Live your magic, as you have the key to unlock time and be magnificent. Blessed be to each of you reading this book right now, as the powers of the forlorn are opened and unleashed to magnify your soul to the son of God within. Blessings to all.
Thank you, Nostradamus!
Thank you, Albert Einstein. Sir Isaac and Nostradamus, I am deeply honored and blessed to be a communicator for each of you, separately, and together. This is fantastic!

Thank you so, my dear, for your work. It is uncanny, to say the least. We are fortunate for your existence, as if not, we would not be able to be a part of our future line of heritage and articulators.

On this day, we shall all join in with Andrea Elizabeth and pronounce that today is the 14th day of self-healing, self-appraisal, self-reliance, and self-control. We ask that all our guides, masters, ascended masters, and higher selves, as well as masters Nostradamus, Albert Einstein, and Sir Isaac, to all come together in a healing bubble of light, self-assessment, and altruistic sight. We give here, in this bubble of hope, a kind and thoughtful self-appraisal of love. We each bring in love from our own time and our own heart to diversify this total and complete encounter. The illusion of time is just that, an illusion. We are all standing here, in this bubble of non-linear time, to complete the 14-day self-healing work and to strengthen each of our faiths to the point of self-acknowledgement, self-reliance, and God reliance. We are the masters of ourselves, and on this day we know it.

We are each permanently changed because of this work that has been done, and we each and all together congratulate you on your journey to enlightenment. The next 7 days will be your own inner journey to enlightenment, and we shall now call upon Master Buddha for your assistance. Blessed be!

My Day 14 Soul Goal is:
Thought for the day:

Today I am healing and hopeful. May I live this way forevermore.

Master Buddha has words for the next 7-day journey to enlightenment

Greetings, Master Buddha, I thank you for your presence on this day.

You are too gracious, my dear, our opulence is in dire need of respect so as we each bring in bits of light your own particles of desire shall enhance.

Master Buddha writes:

Dearest friends, neighbors, brothers, and sisters, you are all welcome here in our circle. Young, old, manifested, non-manifested, old timeline, new timeline, you-name-it. We are all a version of each other, and time is just an illusional concept, if not phenomenal. Each aspect of the son of God, man, or universe keeps each of us on our toes about life.

Here in death, we on this side of the earthly veil remit our kindest thoughts to you and to your own higher version of you, as us. I speak of us in terms of me, as the entire concept of separation is nominal here. No one ever discusses it, as we are all at the same level in the hierarchy. We revel nowhere, for nothing in alwaysness. We are simply, truth be told, a single being of light vibration that permeates and will forevermore glide through the terms of time in such a way that each miniscule space of turmoil is lessened by each and every light-being imaginable.

As the weather on earth seems to be in turmoil, or inner religious, or inharmonious allies, or guidance that is or have been misconstrued by a human being, we terminally remain in our reside here, there, and everywhere, doubting an insurmountable effort to become linear. Meaning that, as one non-believer becomes a believer, or a determiner of the enlightened Buddha or lantern of Christ, a new vibration in the universe is, or becomes, a terse adventure for the relics of the past, as they see the turn of the tides, so to speak, and become an alliance with that version of you. Then, as we all ruminate together as one soul song, our magnificence aligns with the heavens, and the tides turnover to our song, and the irrelevant become relevant, and you become God. It is a song made in heaven, for heaven, by heaven. The heavenly spheres of the Christ lineage or the God consciousness, or the Tao, or Confucius, or whatever you were told to call a religion or belief, are co-mingled, co-created, and co-written with you as us and the God-creation energy.

This is the true and simple fact: God is all things in heaven. God is not a man; God is a singular vibratory light that resides deep within each and every single living being. We harmonize so deeply together in this realm of vibration as a sound of a song. The multitude of caravans throughout the universe know when one begins to find this eternal sight or light within. The multinational universal gong of space is struck, and the eternal gratitude begins.

Here, when we reach deeply inside with the most eternal gratitude known to man, we begin to live again—fully, exceptionally and, finally, rationally. We know that deep inside of us is everything, and as we learn that we are everything, we begin to live by allowing everything into our space, and we find the golden gift of magical livingness, or the beingness, or the knowingness. We begin to imagine that absolutely every single thing we have ever wanted or wished for is attainable.

All throughout history, many on earth have attained very little because of this lack of knowledge. The people found and worshiped icons, such as a specific deity, or money, or religion, or material wealth. They found something other than what was hidden deep within their main crevice of life. This material possession became their eternal God, and all in all, when they died, they took nothing with them. As much as the Egyptians tried to put their chariots and gold into their tombs, it was still there after their death. Furthermore, even if we could imagine taking our material wealth with us in death, it would be of no use, as once you got to the other side, it would have been a futile existence.

After death, one would only find that the imaginary happiness brought on by the old family wealth would be eliminated, and the essence of your own trueness would be immaculate and divine. What is to behold on the other side is that you are the wealth. You are the magic. You are the magnificence of the vibration of a holy, loving God or creator. Each and every human is a luminary child of God.

Today, we add all of this wholeheartedly for you to fully and faithfully bring thanks to your honorary work with Andrea Elizabeth, as well as the masters who have come forward to assist you on your journey to enlightenment. On this day and the days to come, we bequeath to you a very difficult task, the sometimes impossible task of self-forgiveness in all of its glory. You can, and will, become self-reliant on the basis of how much you are able to self-forgive. We will be here with you in this time period bubble, to create a wealth of duties for you to partake in for the next 7 days.

Each duty will be a little more difficult, but worth every second that you put into this daily work with fortitude and grace. Allow us all to be with you and to bequeath to you our own magical assessments of your own self. If you are having difficulty, put your pen down, and call on us to provide you with the assistance you require. It will be quick and simple. Do your best to know this, as life is not complicated; only humans complicate life. On the other side, there are no complications, only simplification. There is no struggle, there is no fighting, it is a sheer longing for the next magnificent moment to come, as each moment outdoes the last.

Now imagine creating that here on earth, and not having to really transition over to the other side to find this. Heaven is what you make of it, here on earth, and when you realize this, you find Nirvana, a place of light, love, and insurmountable grace. Grace flows and flows, simply by living. There is never to be a dark place again, and the reliance upon our creator vibration lights the way to simplicity and, therefore, Nirvana. Nothing less. The divine inside lives and breathes breathlessly, in and through our vibration of God deep within. This space is where your glory lives and resides. Not out there. This vibration is such a deep inside infiltration that we rarely see a human being finding this space. It is a space of true opulence and a grand assurance of peace, love, and enlightenment. As I speak of enlightenment, I will do my best to show you the process.

For the next 7 days, the process will be a little more elite. The elitist is a good way to word it. Your own true way to Nirvana is through the enlightenment process. Each step is a slow process of self-assessment, even further, and self-alignment deeply within, and self-envisioning. Who is it you wish to be at the end of this working process? The telegraphs are off the charts, whizzing away at this. We see you fulfilling your life-long dream of unilaterally becoming your dream magnified, and each step you take puts you closer to your dream of becoming magnificent. And becoming a brilliant glorified magnification of yourself deeply within the reside of your soul. Living from a space of glorified magnification, you accomplish absolutely anything you set your ultimate mind to. Now remember, your ultimate mind is not your head, your ultimate mind is your soul, at your true gut level. This is where you really reside, about two inches behind and below your heart space, in the crevice of time. Here is where the real living begins. This is your timepiece to eternity. Let's get started.

Chapter 17

Day 15 – The Journey of Self-Enlightenment

Our Song of Creation

My journey to self-enlightenment With Master Buddha and Divine Master Kwan Yin

Prayer 21: Opening Prayer

I, along with all my own masters, guides, and journeymen, do hereby switch from clinging to the old and relying on the new. A new embellishment of faith, a new involvement in life, and a true master's journey to the enlightenment of self. I am solely and souly ready for a new life. Now is day 15, I am ready for the next 7 days to be life-changing, breathtaking, and hereby manageable by you all here with me.

Together as one, I have found a new enlightenment in the way I am beginning to think. This is not a singular thought of just me any longer; it is a joyful thought of us. We are together, we are never alone, and I always have someone to call upon for assistance. This is my way of mastery, this is my way of being, and this is my new way of enlightenment. And once and for all, I am a winner at this game of life, not an onlooker or a bystander. I create life, I live life. I am life altogether, as one magnificent light and harmonious vibration of creation. I magnify the universe, and the universe magnifies me. We are solid, and magical, and eternal until the end of time, whenever that may be, and on to Nirvana, with the stars and the masters who have passed over and have helped me on my journey here today.

On this is day 15, we will be working within the realm of the unladen. Free from all burdens, freedom at its finest. We have somewhat cleared away the debris that followed us around and kept us heavy and perhaps even hateful at the guise of life. What we didn't know is that we were most times angry at ourselves having absolutely no knowledge of it. I read today that anger is really disappointed hope, and this so struck a chord in me, as this disappointed hope also causes depression. And depression is caused by anger. So this is where we will begin today.

What has been your biggest disappointment in your life thus far?

Let's list as many here as we can and really get to the heart of our disappointed hopes. Create a list from as far back as you can remember. Just begin and list them, all of them. Good, bad and indifferent. Whatever comes to mind. Then, close the pages.

Return to it tomorrow, or whenever you are ready. The key idea here is to list these angers and resentments, and get them out of your being, as they are blocking the true light of your nature of your God self. Living under all these false pretenses or guises of fake smiling, fake living, and false being keeps you down, covered, and under wraps. We should be able to shine and to allow or own golden God center or center of creation to be felt, heard, and sung. We can never have enough songs to sing. We can never have enough vibrations to feel or to be felt. We can never have enough breath to sing our song of hope. Ever! We have been so disillusioned and dismantled by our own unhappiness that we never really allowed ourselves to live or to be heard or to be seen. We kept our masks on in order to, say, unlive our life. We never felt as though we even deserved to survive.

This day, is going to literally be the first day of discovering, uncovering, and then discarding the old messages, the old ideas, and the old you. My friend, here together with all of our friends, guides, and masters, we all wish to welcome you home. Welcome home to Nirvana, where only peace, love, and enlightenment exist. And as master Buddha stated, we are all one. We are all here to assist you with your list, and we are all here to begin to allow you to vibrate your song of eternity. Life is meant to be lived. We are all going to live it, to the fullest. Together! Are you ready?

Let's create together a list in time periods of 5s.

Let's begin from the time in the womb, to 5 years old, to create a list of disappointments and/or disappointed hopes in your life that made you angry or hurt. In doing this, we are going to find out exactly where the anger lies and where your hope ended. Simply sit, get quiet, and prepare. You can put in earplugs, so quiet all your surroundings, and keep quiet inside and able to listen from that quiet place within that has all the answers. Here is your questionnaire answer-giver. When you are ready, begin, sit in a quiet position, chant the word OM three times, directly from that space behind your heart, and place two fingers below your heart.

This is the opening of Nirvana for you. We are going into Nirvana to dig out the deepest buried lies we have told ourselves, to uncover our own hope, and our own happiness, and our own source of Nirvana. We are going to free ourselves from the past, and begin a new journey to enlightenment, with us as a true source of light. This exercise is going to recover the hidden parts of our soul to such an extent that when we are completely done with this list, we are going to be blown away at what really comes to light. We have been hiding our truths about our lives under a sheer false picture of ourselves. How can it be that all of these years we have sought outwardly, when the true potential to peace was within?

A few examples could be:
- At 5 years of age, my father kept telling me he would play catch with me, but he never was home to do it. He kept giving me false hope about the next time he was home we would play, but we never did.
- When my mother had another child, she said that we would play together and be friends. But my sister didn't want to play boy games, and I really never had a friend.
- My parents got a divorce.
- A parent died.
- I was promised a dog as a kid, but each year came and went, and I never got one.

Let's begin:
- From womb to age 5 years:
- 5 to 10 years old:
- 10 to 15 years old:
- 15 to 20 years old:
- 0-5/5-10/10-15/15-20/ etc.; you get the picture.

Create your list now and then allow it to be in the bubble of Nirvana. Put it away until you are ready for the next step.

In this exercise, we are looking for that disappointed hope in our life, where we can now recognize our anger, hate, and disappointment in each situation. This may be an ongoing process for you, but do the best you can to find all the unanswered questions about this.

In each written answer, jot down a little survival skill you used to get over it.

- What did you seemingly tell yourself about the situation?
- Did you create a story about it and believe it? Did you create a fake friend to play with?
- Did you insist that each and every day your dad would come back home, and he would play ball with you?

Yes, we are looking for the patterns of disappointed hope, but also the patterns of how we coped or survived. Many of us were peacekeepers and didn't want to create waves so we were silent or unseen. So many of us felt unanswered, or unacknowledged, or on the other side, we created chaos, tantrums, and demanded attention. Whatever... We are looking for that deep feeling you had when your hope was taken away, and you became dismantled.

Master Buddha says we brought you to this point of almost sheer despair in order for you to find out that you had a rough going here and yet you managed to somehow find us. We have sheer delight and honor that you are here with us and Andrea Elizabeth today. With this list, we are all going to be accentuating the goodness about you. As you have found the old you, you can also find a new you. There are always solutions at all times, here on the other side of the veil.

We bring into fruition here with you a bittersweet mantra for healing:
- I suffer, therefore I am.
- I have pain, therefore I am alive.
- I falter, therefore I am human.

These three lines are tantamount to show and enhance your kindness about you, and your thoughts and your own valor of the Christ within. In terms of hatred toward others, there can and may be a new trend arising

As in knowing our own weaknesses, we can find our own kindness. We found that our very trueness or truth of our self is deeper inside than any hate we could hold within. We find that to quickly view our unanswered hope is a new way of living, seeing, and being. We always had hope but it was never elevated. As we keep doing this inner work, we are sometimes aghast at the newness of our sight. It is almost as though we have a new set of eyes, yet we have not had eye surgery. We have, however, switched our view of ourselves from the head to our own heart's Nirvana sight. And living in here, in this part of the calibrated brain of our soul, we can finally imagine a life of light all around us. We can finally begin to imagine freedom at its finest by simply being Christ like inside and wholly (and holy) bringing in Nirvana to our sight. As we manage to live from this eyesight from the 3rd chakra sight, we naturally find a vision of God deep within. Which no one can touch. It is ours. It

We bring into fruition here with you a bittersweet mantra for healing:
- I suffer, therefore I am.
- I have pain, therefore I am alive.
- I falter, therefore I am human.

These three lines are tantamount to show and enhance your kindness about you, and your thoughts and your own valor of the Christ within. In terms of hatred toward others, there can and may be a new trend arising

As in knowing our own weaknesses, we can find our own kindness. We found that our very trueness or truth of our self is deeper inside than any hate we could hold within. We find that to quickly view our unanswered hope is a new way of living, seeing, and being. We always had hope but it was never elevated. As we keep doing this inner work, we are sometimes aghast at the newness of our sight. It is almost as though we have a new set of eyes, yet we have not had eye surgery. We have, however, switched our view of ourselves from the head to our own heart's Nirvana sight. And living in here, in this part of the calibrated brain of our soul, we can finally imagine a life of light all around us. We can finally begin to imagine freedom at its finest by simply being Christ like inside and wholly (and holy) bringing in Nirvana to our sight. As we manage to live from this eyesight from the 3rd chakra sight, we naturally find a vision of God deep within. Which no one can touch. It is ours. It

In each written answer, jot down a little survival skill you used to get over it.

- What did you seemingly tell yourself about the situation?
- Did you create a story about it and believe it? Did you create a fake friend to play with?
- Did you insist that each and every day your dad would come back home, and he would play ball with you?

Yes, we are looking for the patterns of disappointed hope, but also the patterns of how we coped or survived. Many of us were peacekeepers and didn't want to create waves so we were silent or unseen. So many of us felt unanswered, or unacknowledged, or on the other side, we created chaos, tantrums, and demanded attention. Whatever... We are looking for that deep feeling you had when your hope was taken away, and you became dismantled.

Master Buddha says we brought you to this point of almost sheer despair in order for you to find out that you had a rough going here and yet you managed to somehow find us. We have sheer delight and honor that you are here with us and Andrea Elizabeth today. With this list, we are all going to be accentuating the goodness about you. As you have found the old you, you can also find a new you. There are always solutions at all times, here on the other side of the veil.

is me. It is you. It is God. It is Nirvana at its finest. Quaint, clear, concise, and heavenly, and all within you. Who knew this was inside us? Certainly not I. As I write this, the Buddha and Divine Master Kwan Yin have been circling like hawks, waiting for me to complete this writing and get it out. "People need their soul," they both say. It is a term of endearment, yes, but a sincere one. All Gods are waiting to be extricated from within. The holy matrimony waits to begin.

In you, in me, in us. We are alive with the magic of light within. And this is our next journey.

My Day 15 Soul Goal is:
Thought for the day:
Today, I live rich in Nirvana. May I live this way forevermore.

Chapter 18
Day 16 – The Enrichment of Your Soul With Master Buddha, our Blessed Mother, and Divine Master Kwan Yin

As I sit here to write this next piece, Master Buddha asks me, "What is your enrichment of your soul today, at this moment? How may you define it? How does it ruminate deeply, and what is the sheer cause of your soul's enrichment?"

Well, I was sort of taken aback at these questions. Really, I am the one writing, but he says we all share our commonalities to exist with each other. So, if I am truly answering for us all, I will say: At this moment, the enrichment of my soul is a derivative of a past stale living. I have had tremendous disappointed hopes, abused others, been abused, been lied to, lied, all the human things that we do. But the absolute most enlightening thing to my soul this day is the manufacturing of the peace within that comes to me from my guides, and the holiness that comes from my knowing. In my knowing, I find that the more I begin to trust, and ask questions, and follow my guided directions, I keep attaining a higher level of, say, advancement, or enlightenment, or Nirvana.

So many words of description, but I do my absolute best to flow the earthly God medicine or God message as best I can, through my own holy chalice as a duty to the heavens, or to God, or to Christ. I wish there were not so many words for everything, and that one simple word would suffice, but I find it so unmanageably difficult to find just one word to surmount the intelligible meaning of "Thy will, not mine, be done." Well, that sort of sums it all up. As I sit with this, I am channeling as best as I can, so that this information is free and pure, and as magical as it can be. I feel so honored to be such a chalice for Christ that I still cry about it. The holy peace I seem to have and to keep having is solely because I live truth, and that I know. That is it; it comes so easily to me, but I assure you that I know, therefore I am.

That is my simple wish to give to you. Know and be. And this is where I believe these writings are from and who they are for. They are for you to get to your own knowing of your own inner God or Christ. For you to know and therefore be.

So let's believe or sit with the understanding for a moment that you know you are God. What next? Well, nothing. That's the superfluous answer we all seek. And because we know this, we are finally able to do the following:

Knowing I am God, I can:
Knowing I am God, I am:
Knowing I am God, I find that:
Knowing I am God, I know:
Knowing I am God, I sound:
Knowing I am God, I create:
Knowing I am God, I realize:
Knowing I am God, I am knowing.

Isn't this fun? Create your own mantra to get to the real inner crux of your soul. Sit at that space behind your 3rd chakra and know. I used to say all the time, in this area of my soul, be still and know that I am God. But, I never really knew why, until I am writing this right now. Oh, my God, what an epiphany! I know now, what I was looking for all those years ago. For over 10 years, my morning meditation or mantra was to sit with my hands on my solar plexus or 3rd chakra, and say to myself, "Be still, and know that I am God." And I would feel an energy and begin to behold these words and really begin to actually believe them. And as I write this here today with all of you, I truly believe that I am God. Now. Nirvana found. Literally, drop the mic. What a revelation to me! Thank you, all who read this, as we are all doing this together on this day as one. This is as much for me as for you. Together we are fighters. As I always say, I don't lose. Period. That's it. I don't lose. Thank you all for finding Nirvana with me. Wow! Ok! Moving on.

So let's say our prayer for this day, together with all the masters: Master Buddha, Master Jesus, Mother Mary, and Divine Master Kwan Yin

Prayer 22

Dear family of one, on this, day 16, we master our knowing of our own inner soul. Our soul's enrichment is one of deep reliance upon our own knowing of our own holy mantra that resides deep within us, as well as our own frequency of our soul remnants that are as holy as the masters themselves.

We pray for the ultimate in enlightenment and for the enrichment of our single soul being, to become a triad within the nations of light.

We ask again to further gain additional knowledge and access to our soul through the heavenly doors of Nirvana.

We stay with you forevermore, from this day on. Blessed be. As the synchronicities of the Holy Christ begin to sing our song as one on this day, the holy magnificence is drawn down unto you this day, and each and every day forward.

Your mantra for this day: I am my own king or queen inside; I brighten my own day; I enlighten my own soul, together as one with the masters. Amen. I Illume.

My day 16 soul goal is:

Thought for the day:

Today I am deeply loved and respected. May I live this way forevermore.

Chapter 19

Day 17 – The Road to Enlightenment Through Nirvana With Master Jesus and Master Buddha

A holy matrimony of delightful light, love, and shared imagination by and through each Holy master. The Holy masters wish to take this time to share fully with each of you their own way to, and of their own mastery, of faith on to Nirvana through enlightenment.

Master Jesus is first:

All are gathered on this holy day of matrimony in a sort of bilateral reunification of our two souls. As we come to master one part of our soul, another one manages to pop up to say hello. That being said, we are multifaceted beings living in a difficult diversion of haste. So many brothers and sisters racing around to be where? Stuck. I bring to you on this day a simile of haste.

And I ask my brothers and sisters: "What is your haste about? Why have you come so far, with so far still to go, for only so little? Have you had much enjoyment? What kind of heart magic have you found through your own ways or terms? Have you had enlightenment?"

Master Buddha chimes in:
Master Jesus, in seeking enlightenment, first seek solace. One's haste has more to do with one's solace than a hurrying kind. For instance, if goat curd was forced to follow a timeline of haste, it would not become goat curd. It would become an inedible watery or thickened paste. There must be patience and tolerance, even with the curd. In the same way, the master must contemplate his thoughts. One at a time, slowly, comfortably, and each in his own manner. This is the coefficient of his bilateral existence. Here on earth, we are bilateral, but in Nirvana, we are anti- or trilateral.

Like the sun, the moon, and the planet Earth, each are trilateral, as in a manner of sight. Our operational sight here on earth is linear, but our Nirvana sight is communal. We are able to use the sight of the masters, if possible. As one gains a higher sight of existence, one begins to use the masters as their own sight, and this is what brings on enlightenment.

Mother Mary has words for all this:
Dearly beloved,

It has been shown here, and together with Andrea Elizabeth, that we are all part of the same whole. We give, you give, we sigh, you sigh, all the same virtual reality here on earth and beyond. We give here on this day to all of you reading, and to all future readers, the greatest allowance to be had. We bring in unilaterally, bilaterally, and trilaterally, our own cord of light streaming down your back, deep into your core, forward in and through your sight space, for our own magnification is by and through your own magnification, as we are all one. We are all challenged to emanate now and forever the evidence of the Holy Christed one within. Blessings to all who come, and to all who pass our way in this timeline. We gather for the most awe-inspiring blessings of our time. We shall all overcome the past, step into the future, and be. This is our challenge for you.

Be at peace within, so that you can be at peace without. There is no solace in fright or even hate. The misuse of solace has been, in the past, self-righteous. It is now forgotten, and the derivative of the Christ is you. You are the holy one, you are the fortune from the past. You are the Christ divine within, forevermore.

This is my message to all: We seek no longer, because we have found refuge in thine honor. Blessed be the king. To you in heaven, as so within your own holy being of the Christ. All is well.

Please, all, sit with these words, they are as holy as you are ever going to get. Feel the capacity for change, and enlightenment, and joy, and trust. Be trust. Know trust. Live trust. This is the peace of the Lord above in heaven. All are forgiven and well. Sit with this energy for a bit. There is absolutely no rush.

To me, this energy feels like a billowy pile of flour, and I am a piece of dough being rolled lightly in it. The cool touch of the flour is soft and cold. I feel free in the sanctity of the Holy Blessed Mother. I believe we have been untied and freed from our past sins. All is forgotten. Our bounty lies within. Let us stay in this energy for awhile. Until tomorrow.

Blessings to you all. I am ever so deeply moved that you allow me to be a part of your life here with you and the masters, writing in such a manner of light. Namaste!

Mantra for the day: I am—that I am

My day 17 soul goal is:

Thought for the day:

Today I live in the light and billowing of heaven this day. May I live this way forevermore.

Chapter 20

Day 18 – The Road to Enlightenment Through Nirvana With Archangel Michael, and Master Lento

Day 18, same topic, 4 days left to go. After reading the day before with the masters, I am absolutely awe-inspired. This work is, or was in the past, saved only for the saints or the angels, I thought. What a heavenly experience I am having, and I hope to the heavens that you are as well. Let's come together again on a common inspiration for the new road to enlightenment through Nirvana.

So here we seek a space of sheer reminiscence of the past writings. As we sort of thumb back through our pages and see our soul purpose, we can begin to really enjoy and relax into ourselves. And having peace with our self gives us a new light, in such a manner that we behold anew every day, every minute, and every second. We begin to really recreate ourselves each and every moment of the day by simply being one of these different ideas about our self. And the absolute quotient to this is that the sum of all things, that which was irregular, now become the norm. And we can begin to envision the Pi in our lives. We can literally begin to see the quotients, the equations, and the diversified outcomes each and every time we think a different thought.

Now I would assume this is physics, had I ever taken a physics class, as it seems very much common sense to me. However, I believe, and have always believed, that we are taught to not look back, but to just keep going, never knowing we even have a chance to change things. And I am assuming as I write these words that this is the inspiration for this 21-day relic from the past to the future, onto the heavens above. That each characterization of self, written down here in this book, actualizes a new version of the old and sufficiently requires mass. As again I believe I wrote previously, the equation of matter that $E=MC^2$ as an equivalent in terms of the heavenly realm definition of mass. Each stone unturned gives us the audacity to deny the old and become anew and live renewed until eternity. So I am being told that E=Eternity and that Mass is the collective consciousness times the speed of light, or times 2. So, as once again Einstein gives us his definition of the relativity of mass, the heavens give us the equation to eternity. Who knew? Once again, as I write these words, I am awestruck.

Absolutely, mind is blown! Here I am sitting in my living room on a semi-cloudy October morning, being allowed to be used as a conduit for the Christ. I am simply in awe each and every moment of my life. And I am assuming this is the next work.

Being awestruck. Living your life in such a way that each diverse moment co-creates magic in the next. The nature of God, or Christ, or source, or the universe, or even the universal mind, is one of a never-ending cycle of charismatic forces of divine light. This divine light weighs heavily on each of us as a sort of conscious. Our conscious is our talking force within, and from this consciousness we find it necessary at most times to listen to it. Now questioning this voice, we sometimes are at odds with it. Especially if it is to our perceived advantage: Say the store clerk gives you back $20 accidentally, or you find things in your basket you hadn't paid for as you get to your car outside the store. These sometimes unconscionable ideas come from where? And becoming a comingled trilateral communicator is how you can become a quiet force within. And in having this force within, you will ultimately have this force without.

Force is diversity at its finest. Force is a gravitational pull on your soul's space, where once you begin to listen, sit quietly and have a divine conversation with the universe, you will begin to imagine. And in imagining, you congruently create. And in creating, you ultimately provide. Now, providing can mean many things. You can work at a job to provide for your family. You can be of assistance in your community to provide for the less fortunate. You can provide money to your church as a way of tithing for your church community. All of these are fantastic; however, where is the phenomenal force for yourself? We provide the force outside ourselves for so long that we never imagine finding the force within.

As we entertain this idea of force, we also ascertain an aspect of God within this force. The so-called imaginary force within, or the voice that speaks to you in all things at all times—this is you, you in the aspects of a force of God. This term is only an explanation, as it comes through me. I am sure there many other definitions. I use these words only to get the masters' point through. So imagine a rocket ship and the power or force that is needed to give it a jaunt to the moon. Especially on a wind-filled hurricane day.

Now, that force needs to be mighty and strong, so as to get through any type of weather and "weather the storm." However, in terms of duty or self-assessment, one rarely begins to even ascertain one's own duty to one's own force. So, typically, we find as we look within, there is no force to be sought out, or even had. The terms of "thy power comes from within" almost seem a farce, as one's own duty to self has been altered into a force of non-duty to self, but a forced duty to things outside of our human self.

What we are about to present is a way, or a force of action, unto its own. We will begin to provide you with your own territory of self. You will be allowed to master your own territory for your own self, for your own God, in your own way. We will become a primary source for your good, for your God, for your own way of identifying your force. You will be strong and mighty, and in conjunction with all that has ever been sought. You will be a respite of truth for all. And in this way, you can begin to ascertain beauty, light, and self-adherence to your own self-knowledge, self-respect, and self-duty. I am. Or, I am that I am. Or, I am Christ. Deep within. Simple terms for our own way of being. If we are a jet propulsion-based eternity, why haven't we indulged within? Why have we not journeyed far deep inside to single out our force?

We masters are in deep thought about this. And in some ways, we are deeming this observation lifeless. As though each shell of a man is blind and dimmed and unfound. We bring to you now a formal assertion of holy matrimony of the divine. We eliminate all that WAS to begin living from a place of all that IS. We are your background for Christ. And in this background, we formally begin opening a space for your truth, for your light, for your love, and for your force to be allowed in our universe, here now, and for eternity, and into Nirvana. We allow the light of the past to come forth and be known, lit and preserved for futures to come. We allow all aspects of the Holy

Christed Being to become full and precise and non-divisive. We are your backing force. We are your jet propulsion. We are the highest version of you in Nirvana.

You are already here. We are just here to help you find your way. Masterfully. So we masterfully sit here with you in this space of alliance as we bring in the big guns, so to speak. The big kahuna, the formidable voice of reason. We bring to you the allowance of the Archangel Michael, with all his knowledge and talents, and his grace, for the beauty of how to live so deep within that your own force becomes your own superhuman power. You can, and will, begin to live in such a space or manner that you find it unnecessary to live the old life. Nirvana is heaven-plus. Nirvana is the delightful version of eternity and more. Nirvana is a light to the old you; it is a secret space that has risen within, so you can return home to your space of life. We behold the next journey and/or versions of yourself with Archangel Michael and his risen guides.
Greetings, Archangel Michael!
Greetings, my beloved!
We all thank you for the wonderful welcome and allowance of or own version of finding the Christ within. Blessed be!

We begin by saying that each past version of you coincides with a version of the Christ. Each and every layer of, say, packing, keeps us stricken with fright. From now on, allow the only Christ version of you to behold your day. Step up and out, away from your old turmoil, and into your greatness, all the time. And when you begin to feel down or listless, remain dutiful to your force within, as stating I am God, or I am Christ. I am a force.

Now, using these temperamental and sometimes, or oftentimes, ridiculed words for, say, God or force, one must come to terms with the unilateral forces we have been told or shown. In the Marxist class theory, one's toll is taken upon himself, as he believes not that he is God or the Christ, and he withers away and dies a broken man or soul. And, as if he were to otherwise regain his inner knowledge of the peace-keeping Christ within, he would have been managed into the plight of not only a man of God, but a God of God. And in so many terms here on this planet Earth, most feel not worthy of stating such. However, if we are to really be God and find this force within, we must change our thinking about the Holy Christed Being, or God, or we become unilateral and plain.

The journey to earth as a man or woman was not to be unsaintly or unfathomable as a, say, saint. Not that we are supposed to do so many things that we are christened a so-called saint by the churches, or whoever is in power there.

The journey to earth as a man or woman was not to be un-saintly or an un-Godly human being. We were supposed to be able to do the things that are saintly and become christened by churches as saints, yet very few are ever sought out and called to sainthood, either by themselves or by any of the superpowers here on earth.

Our journey to earth is one of heartfelt reminiscence of the, say, good old days in Nirvana. We hold light. We give light. We are light. We forage around on this earthly plain, with a very dim existence at best. Further down inside our being, knowing there is more, but how or what it is, and if we were to find it, what would be done with it?

Furthermore, our enlightenment status here on earth is a dreary sight for many, as so few even want to take action to do something so very different and out of the ordinary as to change, because the cause outweighs the means, and one stays stuck in un-enlightenment forever. The cycles of their version of hope become even more hopeless, and more illicit, and become a tyrant for the almost-dark forces. The term "dark angel" has its own terms for the latent, but however it is termed here on earth, our only work is to assist in helping you find Nirvana.

In the next chapters, we will illuminate your heart with talks of the most natural ways to conquer the old self. Our journey to the heart space, or center, begins now on the terms of "the rich get richer, and the poorer get poorer." It is all in the journey, my friend. The journey of action. The force is in the doing of the magnificent work with the angels above to become a heartfelt light of our masters above. And we are to fully begin to ascertain the goodness within as a sort of taste of heaven. We will begin now with a short version of the *Our Father* prayer, and even the *Hail Mary* parity, so as to show you the terms that had been set many years ago, but were turned on their ear because of men and their own scarcity of their existence. Their lines of faith were of no matter. When one is in fear and scarcity, nothing else resides within. In finding this truth, you find your force and you find Nirvana.

The best definition we have found is a rendition of the *Lord's Prayer*, as edited by Emmet Fox. We shall put it in here for those who have an earthly idea of God. This will help you to develop the idea of and for those who are already on the same page. We ask that you read it anyway, as its form has to do with the pretext of God and the heightened awareness, and to find Nirvana. The tides are changing, and we are furthering our light, as bequeathed to us by our Heavenly Father.

Hallowed be thy name.

Archangel Michael insists that I add this, so here it is: From *The Sermon on the Mount: The Key to Success in Life* (1934) ISBN 0-06-062862-6.

The Lord's Prayer

The *Lord's Prayer* is the most important of Christian documents. It was carefully constructed with certain ends in view. It is the best-known and most often quoted *Bible* passage, and a common denominator of all Christian churches. Every Christian child is taught the *Lord's Prayer*. Its use probably exceeds all other Christian prayers. Undoubtedly, everyone who is seeking to follow along the way that Jesus led should make a point of using the *Lord's Prayer*, intelligently, every day.

In order to do this, we should understand that the prayer is a carefully constructed organic whole. Many people rattle through it like parrots, forgetful of the warning that Jesus gave us against vain repetitions, and, of course, no one derives any profit from that sort of thing.

The great prayer is a compact formula for the development of the soul. It is designed with the utmost care for a specific purpose—so that those who use it regularly, with understanding, will experience a real change of soul. The only progress is this change, which is what the *Bible* calls being "born again." It is the change of soul that matters. The mere acquisition of fresh knowledge received intellectually makes no change in the soul. The *Lord's Prayer* is especially designed to bring this change about, and, when it is regularly used, it invariably does so.

The more one analyzes the *Lord's Prayer*, the more wonderful is its construction seen to be. It meets everyone's need, just at their own level. It not only provides a rapid spiritual development for those who are sufficiently advanced to be ready, but in its superficial meaning, it supplies the more simple-minded and even the more materially minded people with just what they need at the moment, if they use the prayer sincerely.

The greatest of all prayers was designed with still another purpose in view, quite as important as either of the others. Jesus foresaw that, as centuries went by, his simple, primitive teaching would gradually become overlaid by all sorts of external things that really have nothing whatever to do with it. He foresaw that men who had never known him, relying, quite sincerely, no doubt, upon their own limited intellects, would build up theologies and doctrinal systems, obscuring the direct simplicity of the spiritual message, and actually erecting a wall between God and man. He designed his prayer in such a way that it would pass safely through those ages without being tampered with. He arranged it with consummate skill, so that it could not be twisted, or distorted, or adapted to any man-made system; so that, in fact, it would carry the whole Christ message within it and yet not have anything on the surface to attract the attention of the restless, managing type of person. So it has turned out that, through all the changes of Christian history, this prayer has come through to us uncorrupted and unspoiled.

The first thing that we notice is that the prayer naturally falls into seven clauses. This is very characteristic of the Oriental tradition. Seven symbolizes individual soul, just as the number twelve in the same convention stands for corporate completeness. In practical use, we often find an eighth clause added, "Thine is the kingdom, the power, and the glory," but this, though in itself an excellent affirmation, is not really a part of the prayer. The seven clauses are put together with the utmost care, in perfect order and sequence, and they contain everything that is necessary for the nourishment of the soul. Let us consider the first clause:

Our Father

This simple statement in itself constitutes a definite and complete system of theology. It fixes clearly and distinctly the nature and character of God. It sums up the truth of being. It tells all that man needs to know about God, and about himself, and about his neighbor. Anything that is added to this can only be by way of commentary, and is more likely than not to complicate and obscure the true meaning of the text. Oliver Wendell Holmes said, "My religion is summed up in the first two words of the Lord's Prayer," and most of us will find ourselves in full agreement with him.

Notice the simple, clear-cut, definite statement, "Our Father." In this clause, Jesus lays down once and for all that the relationship between God and man is that of father and child. This cuts out any possibility that the deity could be the relentless and cruel tyrant that is often pictured by theology. Jesus says definitely that the relationship is that of parent and child; not an Oriental despot dealing with groveling slaves, but parent and child. Now we all know perfectly well that men and women, however short they may fall in other respects, nearly always do the best they can for their children. Unfortunately, cruel and wicked parents are to be found, but they are so exceptional as to make a paragraph for the newspapers. The vast majority of men and women are at their best in dealing with their children. Speaking of the same truth elsewhere, Jesus said, "If you, who are so full of evil, nevertheless do your best for your children, how much more so will God, who is altogether good, do for you?" And so he begins his prayer by establishing the character of God as that of the perfect father dealing with his children.

Note that this clause, which fixes the nature of God, at the same time fixes the nature of man, because if man is the offspring of God, he must partake of the nature of God, since the nature of the offspring is invariably similar to that of the parent. It is a cosmic law that like begets like. It is not possible that a rosebush should produce lilies, or that a cow should give birth to a colt. The offspring is, and must be, of the same nature as the parent; and so, since God is divine spirit, man must essentially be divine spirit, too, whatever appearances may say to the contrary.

Let us pause here for a moment and try to realize what a tremendous step forward we have taken in appreciating the teaching of Jesus on this point. Do you not see that at a single blow, it swept away

99 percent of all the old theology, with its avenging God, its chosen and favorite individuals, its eternal hellfire, and all the other horrible paraphernalia of man's diseased and terrified imagination? God exists, and the eternal, all-powerful, all-present God is the loving father of mankind.

If you would meditate upon this act, until you had some degree of understanding of what it really means, most of your difficulties and physical ailments would disappear, for they are rooted and grounded in fear. The underlying cause of all trouble is fear. If only you could realize to some extent that omnipotent wisdom is your living, loving father, most of your fears would go. If you could realize it completely, every negative thing in your life would vanish away, and you would demonstrate perfection in every phase. Now you see the object that Jesus had in mind when he placed this clause first.

Next we see that the prayer says not "My Father," but "Our Father," and this indicates, beyond the possibility of mistake, the truth of the brotherhood of man. It forces upon our attention at the very beginning the fact that all men are indeed brethren, the children of one father; and that "there is neither Jew nor Greek, there is neither bond nor free, there is neither chose nor unchosen," because all men are brethren. Here, in making his second point, ends all the tiresome nonsense about a "chosen race," about the spiritual superiority of any one group of human beings. He cuts away the illusion that the members of any nation, or race, or territory, or group, or class, or color, are, in the sight of God, superior to any other group. A belief in the superiority of one's own particular group, or "herd," as the psychologists call it, is an illusion to which mankind is very prone, but in the teaching of Jesus, it has no place. He teaches that the thing that places a man is the spiritual condition of his own individual soul, and that as long as he is upon the spiritual path, it makes no difference whatever to what group he belongs, or does not belong.

The final point is the implied command that we are to pray not only for ourselves, but for all mankind. Every student of truth should hold the thought of the truth of being for the whole human race for a least a moment each day, since none of us lives to himself or dies to himself; for indeed we are all truly—and in a much more literal sense than people are aware—limbs of one body.

Now we begin to see how very much more than appears on the surface is contained in those simple words "Our Father." Simple—one might almost say innocent—as they look, Jesus has concealed within them a spiritual explosive that will ultimately destroy every man-made system that holds the human race in bondage.

Which Art In Heaven

Having clearly established the fatherhood of God and the brotherhood of man, Jesus goes on to enlarge upon beings. He cuts away the illusion that the members of any nation, or race, or territory, or group, or class, or color, are, in the sight of God, superior to any other group. A belief in the superiority of one's own particular group, or "herd," as the psychologists call it, is an illusion to which mankind is very prone, but in the teaching of Jesus, it has no place. He teaches that the thing that places a man is the spiritual condition of his own individual soul, and that as long as he is upon the spiritual path, it makes no difference whatever to what group he belongs, or does not belong.

The final point is the implied command that we are to pray not only for ourselves, but for all mankind. Every student of truth should hold the thought of the truth of being for the whole human race for a least a moment each day, since none of us lives to himself or dies to himself; for indeed we are all truly—and in a much more literal sense than people are aware—limbs of one body.

Now we begin to see how very much more than appears on the surface is contained in those simple words "Our Father." Simple—one might almost say innocent—as they look, Jesus has concealed within them a spiritual explosive that will ultimately destroy every man-made system that holds the human race in bondage.

Which Art In Heaven

Having clearly established the fatherhood of God and the brotherhood of man, Jesus goes on to enlarge upon

99 percent of all the old theology, with its avenging God, its chosen and favorite individuals, its eternal hellfire, and all the other horrible paraphernalia of man's diseased and terrified imagination? God exists, and the eternal, all-powerful, all-present God is the loving father of mankind.

If you would meditate upon this act, until you had some degree of understanding of what it really means, most of your difficulties and physical ailments would disappear, for they are rooted and grounded in fear. The underlying cause of all trouble is fear. If only you could realize to some extent that omnipotent wisdom is your living, loving father, most of your fears would go. If you could realize it completely, every negative thing in your life would vanish away, and you would demonstrate perfection in every phase. Now you see the object that Jesus had in mind when he placed this clause first.

Next we see that the prayer says not "My Father," but "Our Father," and this indicates, beyond the possibility of mistake, the truth of the brotherhood of man. It forces upon our attention at the very beginning the fact that all men are indeed brethren, the children of one father; and that "there is neither Jew nor Greek, there is neither bond nor free, there is neither chose nor unchosen," because all men are brethren. Here, in making his second point, ends all the tiresome nonsense about a "chosen race," about the spiritual superiority of any one group of human the nature of God, and to describe the fundamental facts of existence. Having shown that God and man are parent and child, he goes on to delineate the function of each in the grand scheme of things. He explains that it is the nature of God to be in heaven, and of man to be on earth, because God is cause, and man is manifestation. Cause cannot be expression, and expression cannot be cause, and we must be careful not to confuse the two. Here, heaven stands for God or cause, because in religious phraseology, heaven is the term for the presence of God. In metaphysics, it is called the absolute, because it is the realm of pure unconditioned being, of archetypal ideas. The word "earth" means manifestation, and man's function is to manifest or express God, or cause. In other words, God is the Infinite and perfect cause of all things; but cause has to be expressed, and God expresses himself by means of man. Man's destiny is to express God in all sorts of glorious and wonderful ways. Some of this expression we see as his surroundings; first, his physical body, which is really only the most intimate part of his embodiment; then his home; his work; his recreation; in short, his whole expression. To express means to press outwards, or bring into sight that which already exists implicitly. Every feature of your life is really a manifestation or expression of something in your soul.

Some of these points may seem at first to be a little abstract, but since it is misunderstandings about the relationship of God and man that lead to all our difficulties, it is worth any amount of trouble to correctly understand that relationship. Trying to have manifestation without cause is atheism and materialism, and we know where they lead. Trying to have cause without manifestation leads man to suppose himself to be a personal God, and this commonly ends in megalomania and a kind of paralysis of expression.

The important thing to realize is that God is in heaven and man is on earth, and that each has his own role in the scheme of things. Although they are one, they are not one-and-the-same. Jesus establishes this point carefully when he says, "Our Father, which art in heaven."

Hallowed Be Thy Name

In the *Bible*, as elsewhere, the "name" of anything means the essential nature or character of that thing, and so, when we are told what the name of God is, we are told what His nature is, and His name or nature, Jesus says, is "hallowed." Now what does the word "hallowed" mean? Well, if you trace the derivation back into Old English, you will discover a most extraordinarily interesting and significant fact. The word "hallowed" has the same meaning as "Holy," "whole," "wholesome," and "heal," or "healed"; so we see that the nature of God is not merely worthy of our veneration, but it is complete and perfect— altogether good. Some very remarkable consequences follow from this. We have agreed that an effect must be similar in its nature to its cause, and so, because the nature of God is hallowed, everything that follows from that cause must be hallowed or perfect, too. Just as a rosebush cannot produce lilies, so God cannot cause or send anything but perfect good. As the *Bible* says, "The same fountain cannot send forth both sweet and bitter water." From this it follows that God cannot, as people sometimes think, send sickness or trouble, or accidents—much less death—for these things are unlike His nature. "Hallowed be thy name" means "Thy nature is altogether good, and thou art the author only of perfect good." Of purer eyes than to behold evil, and can not look on iniquity.

If you think that God has sent any of your difficulties to you, for no matter how good a reason, you are giving power to your troubles, and this makes it very difficult to get rid of them.

Thy Kingdom Come, Thy Will Be Done, On Earth As It Is In Heaven

Man, being the manifestation or expression of God, has a limitless destiny before him. His work is to express, in concrete definite form, the abstract ideas with which God furnishes him, and in order to do this, he must have creative power. If he did not have creative power, he would be merely a machine through which God worked—an automaton. But man is not an automaton; he is an individualized consciousness. God individualizes Himself in an infinite number of distinct focal points of consciousness, each one quite different, and therefore each one is a distinct experience of knowing the universe. Notice carefully that the word "individual" means undivided. The consciousness of each one is distinct from God and from all others, and yet none are separated. How can this be? How can two things be one, and yet not one and the same? The answer is that in matter, which is finite, they cannot, but in spirit, which is infinite, they can. With our present limited, three-dimensional consciousness, we cannot see this, but intuitively, we can understand it through prayer. If God did not individualize Himself, there would be only one experience; as it is, there are as many universes as there are individuals to form them through thinking.

"Thy kingdom come" means that it is our duty to be ever occupied in helping to establish the kingdom of God on earth. That is to say, our work is to bring more onto this plane. That is what we are here for. The old saying, "God has a plan for every man, and he has one for you," is quite correct. God has glorious and wonderful plans for every one of us. He has planned a splendid career, full of interest, life, and joy, for each, and if our lives are dull, or restricted, or squalid, that is not his fault, but ours.

If only you will find out the thing God intends you to do, and will do it, you will find that all doors will open to you, all obstacles in your path will melt away, you will be acclaimed a brilliant success, you will be most liberally rewarded from the monetary point of view, and you will be gloriously happy.

There is a true place in life for each one of us, upon the attainment of which we shall be completely happy, and perfectly secure. On the other hand, until we do find our true place, we never shall be either happy or secure, no matter what other things we may have. Our true place is the one place where we can bring the kingdom of God into manifestation, and truly say, "Thy kingdom cometh."

We have seen that man too often chooses to use his free will in a negative way. He allows himself to think wrongly, selfishly, and this thinking brings upon him all his troubles. Instead of understanding that it is his essential nature to express God, to be ever about his father's business, he tries to set out upon his own account. All our troubles arise from just this folly. We abuse our free will, trying to work apart from God, and the very natural result is all the sickness, poverty, sin, trouble, and death that we find on the physical plane. We must never for a moment try to live for ourselves, or make plans or arrangements without reference to God, or suppose that we can be either happy or successful if we are seeking any other end than to do His Will.

Whatever our desire may be, whether concerning our daily work, or our duty at home, our relations with our fellowman, or private plans for the employment of our own time, if we seek to serve self instead of

God, we are ordering trouble, disappointment, and unhappiness, notwithstanding what the evidence to the contrary may seem to be. Whereas, if we choose what, through prayer, we know to be His Will, then we are insuring for ourselves ultimate success, freedom, and joy, however much self-sacrifice and self-discipline it may involve at the moment.

Our business is to bring our whole nature, as fast as we can, into conformity with the Will of God, by constant prayer and unceasing, though unanxious, watching. "Our wills are ours to make them Thine."

"In His Will is our peace," said Dante, and the divine comedy is really a study in fundamental states of consciousness, the Inferno representing the state of the soul that is endeavoring to live without God, the paradise representing the state of the soul that has achieved its conscious unity with the Divine Will, and purgatory is the condition of the soul that is struggling to pass from one state to the other. It was this sublime conflict of the soul that wrung from the heart of the great Augustine the cry, "Thou hast made us for Thyself, and our hearts are restless until they repose in Thee."

In so many words and to perhaps paraphrase, I pass the following:

In order to do this, we should understand that the prayer is a carefully constructed organic whole. Many people rattle through it like parrots, forgetful of the warning that Jesus gave us against vain repetitions,

God, we are ordering trouble, disappointment, and unhappiness, notwithstanding what the evidence to the contrary may seem to be. Whereas, if we choose what, through prayer, we know to be His Will, then we are insuring for ourselves ultimate success, freedom, and joy, however much self-sacrifice and self-discipline it may involve at the moment.

Our business is to bring our whole nature, as fast as we can, into conformity with the Will of God, by constant prayer and unceasing, though unanxious, watching. "Our wills are ours to make them Thine."

"In His Will is our peace," said Dante, and the divine comedy is really a study in fundamental states of consciousness, the Inferno representing the state of the soul that is endeavoring to live without God, the paradise representing the state of the soul that has achieved its conscious unity with the Divine Will, and purgatory is the condition of the soul that is struggling to pass from one state to the other. It was this sublime conflict of the soul that wrung from the heart of the great Augustine the cry, "Thou hast made us for Thyself, and our hearts are restless until they repose in Thee."

In so many words and to perhaps paraphrase, I pass the following:

In order to do this, we should understand that the prayer is a carefully constructed organic whole. Many people rattle through it like parrots, forgetful of the warning that Jesus gave us against vain repetitions, most liberally rewarded from the monetary point of view, and you will be gloriously happy.

There is a true place in life for each one of us, upon the attainment of which we shall be completely happy, and perfectly secure. On the other hand, until we do find our true place, we never shall be either happy or secure, no matter what other things we may have. Our true place is the one place where we can bring the kingdom of God into manifestation, and truly say, "Thy kingdom cometh."

We have seen that man too often chooses to use his free will in a negative way. He allows himself to think wrongly, selfishly, and this thinking brings upon him all his troubles. Instead of understanding that it is his essential nature to express God, to be ever about his father's business, he tries to set out upon his own account. All our troubles arise from just this folly. We abuse our free will, trying to work apart from God, and the very natural result is all the sickness, poverty, sin, trouble, and death that we find on the physical plane. We must never for a moment try to live for ourselves, or make plans or arrangements without reference to God, or suppose that we can be either happy or successful if we are seeking any other end than to do His Will.

Whatever our desire may be, whether concerning our daily work, or our duty at home, our relations with our fellowman, or private plans for the employment of our own time, if we seek to serve self instead of and, of course, no one derives any profit from that.

The *Lord's Prayer* is a compact formula for the development of the soul. It is designed with the utmost care for that specific purpose; so that those who use it regularly, with understanding, will experience a real change of soul. The only progress is this change, which is what the *Bible* calls being born again. It is the change of soul that matters. The mere acquisition of fresh knowledge received intellectually makes no change in the soul. The *Lord's Prayer* is especially designed to bring this change about, and when it is regularly used, it invariably does so.

Mr. Fox states so many wonderful things, "Prayer is a carefully constructed organic whole." So much so that each word undoubtedly feels real and organic. He also states that this "Great Prayer" is a compact formula for the development of the soul. And this is exactly why Archangel Michael had me put it in here. Why would anyone want to reinvent the wheel, when it has already been stated quite honestly and reverently perfect?

I love this following piece so much that I wish to say it again.

"It is designed with the utmost care for the specific purpose; so that those who use it regularly, with understanding, will experience a real change of soul. The only progress is this change, which is what the *Bible* calls being born again. It is the change of soul that matters. The mere acquisition of fresh knowledge received intellectually makes no change in the soul."

And this is the real effigy of the saints, to become usefully and understandingly whole.

So, having read all this, that is the next work. We wish for each of you to become, or have an even further understanding of, what God's will is for you. In present tense, of course. There will be no looking back or forward; we will be asking a simple question.

What is God's will for you right now? And in reading this, I am sure you are saying, "I don't know. I am not God." Oh, but my friend, we are all God. And in this particular version of God that you are, your will is to be determined greatly by the knowingness of your soul. Correct. So let's ask again.

What is God's will for my soul? Now, this is a better question. And to answer this, or give a brief explanation of how to find it, or exacerbate your song within, we allow for the master Sir Lento to step in and demonstrate a journey he once had.

Hello, Sir Lento!

Hello, my lovely! How are you this fine day in October? I am grand and living gracefully in this final moment of time, waiting lovingly for the next grace-filled moment in time.

Oh, I see you have been practicing our gifts. But of course. How could I allow this latent gift to be dishonored any longer? I have just scratched its surface, I feel. I am awe-fully inspired by life today in all its glory and non-glory. For I know now, whatever will be, will be. I live the acceptance of the holy trinity at its finest, and wish to become a natural light in this world, fully opulent and divine.

Well, my dear, you are doing a great job, and coming along swimmingly.

Thank you, Sir Lento!

I come in at a time when your book of faith is almost finished, to be a beacon of light to the heavens above. And as you were writing that *Lord's Prayer* and speaking about it to us, it may be rather difficult to explain the will of God, or a God, or a higher power to some who may be having difficulty reading this text. We often show the world our indelible ways, but do not fully explain them to their own understanding. So I am coming through to influence your teachings with the assistance of all ascended beings, so that each person may begin to facilitate their passages to the next level of their own Nirvana.

You see, there is no ONE place called Nirvana, as each person will have their own respective space. In earthly terms, stating just the word Nirvana, one may begin to ascertain that they have to get to one specific place or one specific Nirvana. So to show Nirvana in terms of our own enlightenment, Nirvana we offer you this:

On such an earthly plain, one may find it necessary to construct a place where he may or may not have to be or reside. It could be in the hollows of this illusion one may find it illusionary to say, be in one place all at once. At one point, he may even begin to fathom his worth or space in terms of his own duty to the Holy Christ within.

Seeking this place within sometimes is a betrayal to the nature of one self, inasmuch as you have been told and prodded to pray this way or do church that way. One may have an exacerbated a rendition of the Christ as an unnatural being within. We bring this up only to simplify that term for some. Nirvana: The realm of the unknown, by Master Lento and the Angelic Realm of the Heavens.

We bring this part in today as an almost unknown depiction of man, or Christ, or the Holy One, as so many authors have depicted their own stations of the cross for their own initiation of the Holy Christed Being. And every once in a while that a person, such as Andrea Elizabeth, is sometimes able to inhabit a space where one feels the need to shower the world with these priceless gifts but has no name to give to it.

And the shallowness of man here on earth, and his proprietary status of seeking to be good or to do well in the name of God or Christ, belittles the name we have given the Holy being. We may call it the Holy atrocity, as for so many years in the name of Christ people have been killed, and slaughtered, and haunted by their past behaviors of the man of Christ. So as a sort of mainstay, we bring here to you this advice to those who are having a hard time reading this. Or have no knowledge of Christ or even Christianity.

So as a mainstay or template for this next work, we convey to you our way of thinking about the Holy Christed Being, or the God within.

We all at our finest hour give to you the utmost respect and valor for even reading up to now. We completely understand that some of these writings have been a bit of a hard read for those to whom the bell has not tolled. In other words, we identify with and to the believers and the non-believers of God, the non-God, the un-God, etc. We here on the other side are the so-called gatekeepers of the planet. So we must be the purveyors of hope for those who struggle with an all-knowing concept. We must begin to ascertain an aspect of the Holy Christ within that is not doubtful to your soul space. One that has either been adulterated, altered by hate or abuse, contained by another, or shed by your spirit as an unholy mass of flesh. With all the un-Godly thoughts about this being true, we are here to convey that you are holy, and you are good, and you have the traits of a survivor, just as many of us do. At some point in our life, we have to contemplate our lives and see where and when they quit working.

For some, it was at an early age, and for some it was later in life. Which is what Andrea Elizabeth was trying to say a few chapters back. Finding where our lives went wrong or awry, our beliefs went wrong, our ideas went wrong. Where we had disappointed hope in our lives. This is the mainstay we wish to convey and bring up as a part of the forgiveness process. Throughout this book, Andrea Elizabeth has tried her best to relay, in the thread of forgiveness in each chapter, digging deeper into your wounds. And as a once-suppressed soul, I shall say she did an allegiance to our suffering, and gave it her best shot. So now, we are here to allow the follow-up to continue.

And I say to you on this day: Deep within the hand of God, you are worthy. Your own ultimate sacrifice of your worthiness to ascertain a life here on earth is all forgiven, and shall remain in the past. New ideas are formed in enlightenment and Nirvana. As we always state, the road to Nirvana is paved with the pain of our past, its open bleeding wounds, and the hidden turmoil of what others may have done to us or to our families. We find strength deep within our own force and within our own souls, in our residing heaven above. We decipher cruelty that has come into a non-issue state. All of our pain is behind us and, as we step over the forbidden line-up and into a secret light that is hidden just below the surface of our feet, we begin to ascertain the privity of home. We are of the nature that home is where the heart is. As above, so below, all are here to ascertain the madness that is earthly life. These workings, and mantras and affirmations that have been written down for you reveal the battalion of the Holy Christed Being. As we stand here today.

ideas went wrong. Where we had disappointed hope in our lives. This is the mainstay we wish to convey and bring up as a part of the forgiveness process. Throughout this book, Andrea Elizabeth has tried her best to relay, in the thread of forgiveness in each chapter, digging deeper into your wounds. And as a once-suppressed soul, I shall say she did an allegiance to our suffering, and gave it her best shot. So now, we are here to allow the follow-up to continue.

And I say to you on this day: Deep within the hand of God, you are worthy. Your own ultimate sacrifice of your worthiness to ascertain a life here on earth is all forgiven, and shall remain in the past. New ideas are formed in enlightenment and Nirvana. As we always state, the road to Nirvana is paved with the pain of our past, its open bleeding wounds, and the hidden turmoil of what others may have done to us or to our families. We find strength deep within our own force and within our own souls, in our residing heaven above. We decipher cruelty that has come into a non-issue state. All of our pain is behind us and, as we step over the forbidden line-up and into a secret light that is hidden just below the surface of our feet, we begin to ascertain the privity of home. We are of the nature that home is where the heart is. As above, so below, all are here to ascertain the madness that is earthly life. These workings, and mantras and affirmations that have been written down for you reveal the battalion of the Holy Christed Being. As we stand here today.

reading this. Or have no knowledge of Christ or even Christianity.

So as a mainstay or template for this next work, we convey to you our way of thinking about the Holy Christed Being, or the God within.

We all at our finest hour give to you the utmost respect and valor for even reading up to now. We completely understand that some of these writings have been a bit of a hard read for those to whom the bell has not tolled. In other words, we identify with and to the believers and the non-believers of God, the non-God, the un-God, etc. We here on the other side are the so-called gatekeepers of the planet. So we must be the purveyors of hope for those who struggle with an all-knowing concept. We must begin to ascertain an aspect of the Holy Christ within that is not doubtful to your soul space. One that has either been adulterated, altered by hate or abuse, contained by another, or shed by your spirit as an unholy mass of flesh. With all the un-Godly thoughts about this being true, we are here to convey that you are holy, and you are good, and you have the traits of a survivor, just as many of us do. At some point in our life, we have to contemplate our lives and see where and when they quit working.

For some, it was at an early age, and for some it was later in life. Which is what Andrea Elizabeth was trying to say a few chapters back. Finding where our lives went wrong or awry, our beliefs went wrong, our

We are one, finally.

Be that as it may, we still will find ourselves hurling through our past. As you catch yourself doing this, stop and state: "We are One. We are stronger together in numbers with all the holy beings by my side. I am never alone."

I reside at home. In enlightenment. In Nirvana. Peace is within, and peace I shall only be. There are no more sorrows, there is no more pain. I have extinguished the guilt over my past, and have forgiven every single human being for their misfortunes of their guilt, and the pain they projected onto me creating pain for me. I no longer live that existence. I live only in the peace of my heart and within the Nirvana I have found. Blessed be to the holy one inside, as so much more has awakened. I reside at peace at home, and at long last, I am free from the old issues of myself. I opt out of the past, and live in each and every graceful moment of life, flowing naturally, easily, and faithfully from one second to the next, one moment to the next, and one lifetime to the next. I am free to be me, exponentially, forevermore. Blessed be. Amen!

Mantra for the Day: I am home.

Thought for the day:

Today I am free to be me, always. May I live this way forevermore.

Chapter 21
Day 19

A world of forgiveness is a world free of pain. But in living in such a world, how can one find life? Well, much has already been said and is beginning to, hopefully, sink in. So as we find our path and begin to live God's will for us, we also begin to find peacc.

In walking in this peace, we have a profound altercation with who we are inside and where we are best at home. And as that as the final conclusion of our living daily, we set out how to ultimately find how to change the path to home as any resistance may cause harmful results inside our great reside.

Here we find that living a life of unmentionables gives us a life of unfathomable. So if we live a life of tremendous light, our life becomes more manageable, meaning that the more right things we do, the better our life is, and the more wrong things, we do the worse our life gets. Common sense, right? Sure, but what if one person has a hungry child to feed but has not enough money? Shall they lie and steal to get it, or tell the truth and suffer? This is a difficult predicament, as one can do both and have the same outcome, but all in all, we believe it is in faith that life comes to fruition. If we so believe that there is a God living so deeply within us, we may or may not find it difficult to ascertain this God and so we keep doing the wrong things, resulting in wrong outcomes.

You may ask, "So what are the right things?" Well we shall begin to wind this book down with daily living aspects of self.

- How much do you really want to live a good life?
- How much do you really want to even practice any of what has been written here?
- What are the best aspects or parts of your days?

Are they when you are quiet, or when you are working and making money, or rearing your children?

- Is it when you are editing and sitting quietly with God, watching your children play, watching your animals play?
- What gives you the most joy in your life today?

Make a list. This list can be as long as you like; take a while to think about it, if you need to.

What aspects of yourself are present during these joyful moments?

- Is it your trusting self?
- Is it your loving self?
- Is it your funny self?

- Is it your kind self?
- Is it your God self?

What we will be trying to do in this chapter is to find the resistance in your life that does not allow you to live your perspective of joy through a God-filled life.

What are your hesitations in living a joy-filled, or God-filled life? Would it mean that you have to stop eating cookies?

Would it mean that you would have to stop working at a back-breaking job? Would it mean that you may have to release those relationships that bring chaos into your life?

There are so many aspects to this work, it often seems sometimes pointless to just try to do it in 21 days. But letting go of what we find here will assist you in finding your own joy, in your own soul, for your own peace. We are no longer here to give away our peace in order to live a joy-filled life. Where have we gone? That is always my question. As I got to the end of my old life, I truly asked myself. How did I get here? And why did I wait so long for joy to be allowed into my life? Here I was, a broken, homeless mother of two, at my wits end with men, and alcohol, and I sat and cried out to God, a God I had never addressed before. But here is what I know about that time: I was so sincere in my heart that there were no blockages, or lies, or non-trust in that cry to God. I was as honest and as open as I could be at the time, and I cried out,

"God, please help me!" The very next day, I was on the road to a new life.

And as I sit here today, it has been 18 years since my cry out to a God I didn't know, and again I ask the question, "How did I get here?" I wrote this book in hopes that my past experience would give you a boost in seeking a change in your lifestyle as it relates to God, hope, faith, and joy. That your soul would grow legs and let your message be heard. I co-created this with all aspects of God in mind, really interpreting to the best of my ability, purity, charity, unselfishness and love—the four absolute hierarchal meanings of God. The truth of the matter is, we are all varying aspects of the Holy Christed Being, and we promisingly rise to the higher vibrational realm and assist from the highest aspect of ourselves. Not the earthly self but the higher, more vibratory self. The frequency of unconditional love expressed as light. The more we rise vibrationally and become fully empowered, the more full and joyful our lives will become. We become the entire aspect of God, who we are at our core. By illuminating ourselves, we illuminate God or the sheer vibration of God. All aspects of good are God. And when we are living a good life, dismantling the old, relieving the pressures of our life in one way or another, we get to be free from the reality of the earthly plain, and begin to distribute light to our own arena that by far is the biggest contemplation I have found. In my arena, I assist souls, and in your arena, you assist souls. Living our lives in an arena gives us the go-ahead to really evaluate our lives and, as we become further enriched by our own source inside, we find our arena grows, both unilaterally and trilaterally, up and out, and beyond the universal realm. As to touch each and every star above. We have finally found the Nirvana we have sought, after all these lifetimes. And in coming to the end of the old part of us, we can further assist others on their journey to the light or to enlightenment or to illuminating others. Whatever your term is, use it! There is no copyright on God, or goodness, or illumination. Be God in all aspects of things to all people, and live the splendid life of illumination.

As a formal introspection of self, I bring up the manmade "7 deadly sins" or human failings: Pride, Anger, Greed, Gluttony, Lust, Envy, and Sloth. Seven ideals of life which, if you look deeply into our current world now, are rampant everywhere. And if I energetically look at this, I feel sick to my stomach. As a seer, I am often purposefully misaligned with the world at large, as it creates a sort of domino effect in my gut. I see rage or greed as I watch the news, or if I am in public, I feel terrible in my core. It has been a journey in itself, having to learn to shield my heart, as my eyes see what my mind does not want to see. So I bring these 7 human failings up as a sort of checklist for your life. I am also going to throw in a 12-step term of self-centered fear. The definition is that we act from a place of fear because we are afraid, either of not getting something we think we deserve, or we lose something we think we possess. I love this, as I have lived that way my entire life. And when something was taken from me or someone I loved left my life, I reacted in fear and thought selfishly to myself, I will never have another couch like that, my house will look a mess, or I will never have another person to love me because I am a piece of crap. As I looked back over my life and found that fear was a horrible corroding influence in my life. I sought to change that. And what I have written about in this book is how I changed the way I lived. I now include these 7 deadly sins and self-centered fear as a sort of checklist for you when you are feeling out of balance.

9-Point Checklist

I often use these as a checklist when I am feeling anxious, or angry, or restless, irritable, or discontent. The "RIDS" we call them. If I am living from a point or moment of unsatisfied demands somewhere in my current situation in which I cannot quite pinpoint why I am feeling diffident, or on edge, or angry, I ask myself, "Is it Pride, Anger, Greed, Gluttony, Lust, Envy, or Sloth? Am I afraid of losing something I think I possess? Or am I afraid of not getting something I think I deserve?" Here is a 9-point checklist before I even have to ask for help from my guides or my higher self. I am privy to this information only because I became an alcoholic, which in actuality means that

I am bodily and mentally different from my fellows, and when I take any form of alcohol in my body, it reacts chemically and creates an excessive thirst that can really never be satisfied.

It is like the diabetic, whose pancreas does not create the enzymes to anticipate the sugar consumption one takes in. And when this happens to a diabetic, it also creates an insatiable thirst for drink, but their desire is for water. And they drink, and they drink, and they drink, but are never satisfied. The same thing happens with me. I know this firsthand, because I saw it in my 24-year-old daughter, who has diabetes. She became very ill and weak, and had general malaise for a few months before Christmas. This was right around the time when we eat Christmas cookies, and sweets, and give each other chocolate as gifts. She was sitting in front of me one day, drinking water, and she kept filling up her cup and drinking. We didn't know at the time that she would end up in the ICU, almost dead from the high levels of sugar in her system.

As I look back, it is the exact same problem I have, but mine relates to alcohol. The difference is that I used alcohol to check out of my life when I had emotional issues, or felt off, or misjudged, or for whatever reason. I was not able to live a life where I was present, period. I needed to check out.

So after I stopped using alcohol as a crutch, I needed to find a new solution, and my solution was primarily God, which I found through the 12 steps of AA. So as I cleared my core of garbage, released my fears, resentments, and harms, as well as poor sexual conduct, I became a free soul.

But I also needed a new crutch or a new belief or set of standards to live by. So when I felt restless, irritable, or discontented, I was given these tools to live free and at peace. I used these tools so much that they became natural practice to me. I had to continually have a conversation with myself about how I was feeling whenever I would feel disillusioned, or angry, or what-have-you. I would stop myself and say, now in this situation, which of the nine variants are you in? I learned to self-examine and then take action to change my feelings or emotions by creating a trustworthy relationship with myself. I did this by beginning to believe that I would consistently make the changed needed to heal.

For much of my life, I would get this uneasiness in my gut, right in my solar plexus, where I believe now that God resides. I believe I lived most of my life unaware of how to actually handle life. So here I give to you the mainstay of my existence, so that you, too, can live free and happy, and in joy all the time. Not that this is a simple fix to your life. But if you have gone through each aspect of self, and completed this work I have presented, this will be the next step for you to have joyous living.

Let's talk about "fear" in all this. Fear is the chief activator of all our character defects. If we are living a fear-based life, as though waiting for the other shoe to drop, or feelings of doom and gloom run our existence, then the fear activates each and every one of our character defects. And we are living in chaos. The more we begin to trust and live in love, happiness, joy, and trust our own creator within, the more we will live a balanced, happy, peaceful life.

I am including the explanations of these 7 deadly sins so you do not have to look elsewhere for them. However, if you find you cannot control one aspect of yourself, ask your guides for more assistance. Use the tools in this book to stop the behavior and try something different. If you continually get angry, do your best to stop yourself and ask, "Why do I keep doing this behavior? Is it Pride, Anger, Greed, Gluttony, Lust, Envy, Sloth, or Self-Centered Fear?"

The more you stop and check yourself, the more you will begin to understand yourself, and the more joy you will find in your life.

Self Check: 9-Point Definitions
- Pride—a feeling, or deep pleasure, or satisfaction derived from one's own achievements; the achievements of those with whom one is closely associated, or qualities, or possessions that are widely admired.
- Anger—a strong feeling of annoyance, displeasure, or hostility.

- Greed—intense and selfish desire for something, especially wealth, power, or food.
- Gluttony—habitual greed, or excess in eating.
- Lust—very strong sexual desire.
- Envy—a feeling of discontented or resentful longing aroused by someone else's possessions, qualities, or luck.
- Sloth—reluctance to work or make an effort; laziness.
- Self-centered Fear—fear of losing something you think you possess, or fear of not getting something you think you deserve.
- Fear—an unpleasant emotion caused by the belief that someone or something is dangerous, likely to cause pain or a threat.

These are our basic human failings—our instincts gone astray—and as you look at the list, FEAR is the most easily accessible to us. It is mostly our go-to emotion. However, if you have faith, then your fear subsides, and if you practice each and every day to use the tools in this book, I can pretty much guarantee you a little reprieve from your emotional hell. Especially the fear. Fear resides in all aspects of our life. Corporations use fear to market to us drugs, food, and emotional well-being, and what-have-you. Society has created a fear-based life, so that we will buy what they are selling. Furthermore, our parents and our grandparents were all raised in a fear-based society, and have passed this down traditionally to us. And that is the exact reason I began to write this book. Well, that, and the pressure from my guides and the universe. But I hope that by now your faith has outgrown your fear in some capacity. You can now manage your life using the tools in this chapter so that you can self-check and then move on. I believe this book is almost a manual for living. So let's do a little more work on these human failings before we move on. Use this checklist and let's identify which ones are prevalent now.

The acronym I use is PAGGLES + Fear:
- Pride
- Anger
- Greed
- Gluttony
- Lust
- Envy
- Sloth
- Fear and self-centered Fear

Take this list and look at your current life situation, or whatever it is that is getting in the way of your living a joy-filled life. It could be a job, relationship, children, parents. or any number of things. Just begin to write a few for now, then as you get the hang of this write more.

Ask yourself, which one, or how many, of the non-characteristics of God are you living in?

Then write about each one. First find the non-characteristic of God behavior, then write the opposite God-like characteristic of it. Use this list as a tool to help you to begin to act and live in the characteristics of God.

First we make a list, then we identify which part of our self is acting out or uncharacteristically as God, then we find the God-like traits, and begin acting as such. This will take awhile, but the more you inventory your daily life and find where you are misunderstood or mistaken in mind, body, and soul, the quicker you will begin acting with God in your life. We must find out what the problem is before we can reconcile it. So check yourself using these self-check tools. Once you begin to encounter yourself in unsatisfactory situations, you will begin to ask yourself why, and this is when you know the process has begun. Characteristics of self and Characteristics of God:

Characteristics of Self	Characteristics of God
Pride	Humility, Modesty, Humbleness, Patience
Anger	Happy, Calm, Contented, Peaceful, Joy
Greed	Self-Sacrificing; Giving to Others
Gluttony	Abstentious, Abstinent, Self-Denying, Temperate
Lust	Aversion for, Strong Dislike, Dread or Avoid, Chastity
Envy	Admiration or Strong Adoration for, Kindness
Sloth	Industrious, Diligent, Hardworking, Conscientious
Self-centered fear	Emotional Balance, Acceptance
Fear	Courage, Trust, Faith, Love

The seven contrary virtues that are opposites of the seven deadly sins:
- Humility against Pride,
- Kindness against Envy,
- Abstinence against Gluttony,
- Chastity against Lust,
- Patience against Anger,
- Liberality against Greed,
- Diligence against Sloth.

So I will end with this. In all of these opposites, we find one main thread—God, or source, or universe is needed to keep us balanced. All equal to trust, and to faith, and to humility. Humility to me is God, as the more I trust and know I am safe and well taken care of, the more I know God is doing the work for me. That way, I no longer have to worry. I live truly and adoringly in knowing that God is. I am predominantly a fully trusting believer in the Holy Christed Being within and, knowing this, I can have solace in that. Also, in doing all of these daily practices, over time they will become a daily living sort of ritual that will become automatic, and I am free to live in the joy of our creator. I am able to live in the joy of me, and I am the holy trinity within. I am all that I am, and knowing this gives me the peace and serenity I adore.

I will finish with my other favorite prayer from AA's 12-step program:

Prayer 23: The Third Step Prayer
God, I offer myself to Thee—to build with me, and to do with me as Thou wilt. Relieve me of the bondage of self,

that I may better do Thy will to those I would help with Thy power, Thy love, and Thy way of life. May I do Thy will always.

I use this often, as it allows me to begin from a position of trust; then I turn my will and my life over to the CARE of God, as I understand God. I do this prayer every day upon awakening, and I wholeheartedly state these words and totally believe in my core that I am taken care of. I'm then allowed to have a fabulous day, without worry. And, yes, things in life do come up, but I believe in the theory of all things in this world are attributed to my own living and are a factor of my behaviors, and my human failings, I create a canvas for God to actually use my humanness as a tool for guiding others. So my point is that I am not perfect, but I believe God is perfect, and the perfection I display on a daily basis adds in the creation of faith, which leads to happiness, joy, and inner light. That way, I am able to live the Godly characteristic of humility, which is a clear recognition of what and who we really are, followed by a sincere attempt to become what we could be, and becoming able to recognize our human defects or human failings is our first step toward attaining humility in our lives.

This to me is the best definition I could ever find, as it states we are in a state of growing and becoming more of who we think God would have us be. But also, in attaining this grace, we begin to acknowledge this presence in our lives as a way to bring some faith into our life. The more we understand and know that God is working in our life for us, we can begin to understand the statement of the father—doeth thy works, not I—and the more we trust this statement, the more we give our self-will away and begin living in the will of God. It is simple, but not easy.

As we begin to ascertain more truths about who we are, who we were, and who we can attain to become, we have a balance of the coveted light within. And within this light-bearing soul we have, we are able to continually and aptly become more of who we wish to be as humans. In all of this, we find our self, which is the greatest gift of all.

Blessed be!

Mantra for the day:

Thought for the day:

Today I am aware of myself, and I am grateful to know me; thy will, not mine, be done. May I live this way forevermore.

Chapter 22

DAY 20 – HUMILITY WITH MASTER JESUS

Humility through the holy endeavor of minesweeping. In looking back at these writings, I find we have uncovered some hidden land mines within. Some were explosive, some were hidden so deeply that we thought they would never come up, and some were simply on the surface, waiting to be defined or demolished.

In this chapter, we choose humility as a topic, as we believe that all roads lead to humility. And with great fortune, we have the master himself with words.

Good morning, Master Jesus!
Good morning, my child!
How are you this day?
We are well, my dear child.
I grieve no longer, as the holy gifted being is rising within us all.
Yes, father.

And each and every temperate step released the old and began anew. Like my stepping from the old stones to a new one—each time, a new beginning. And in this new way of knowing, loving, and being, we can all begin to ascertain a new way of presenting our self to the world through our illuminated light within. We are now a great catch—all for divinity, meaning that with each new way of acting, and with each new way of retraining our brains, we begin to become no longer skeptical when it comes to new beginnings in our life.

Father, may I ask why you keep using the words us and we?

Of course, my dear child. As in the chapters before, we all wrote this book, we all sat with you, waiting for you to appear to be solid in your faith in yourself to write this book. All of the masters circled around you and held your space until you became alive enough to finally know the truth—that we are all one, and we are all our father's children, and we are you, and you are we, without any separation. There is no us, or we, or I, or you. My dear child, we are a conglomeration of the Holy Christed Being within each and every soul here on earth, and that is why, when we see our ailing brothers and sisters, it goes to the depths of our soul, being hurt and pained. So as we write this with you, the new reader will begin to proclaim also that I am we, and we are I, particularly with this piece here. As our own hearts are immaculately divine within, and every single cell and divisionary space within has its new conclusionary vibration of us as we and I. We live here together in each and every soul, and the Holy Christed Being is profoundly existent with this new vibratory sound we have created here.

The heavens sing glory to the praise of our future life here on earth, as we believe each person reading this will have a new profound effect on our galaxy, so as to begin anew once again. Life never really ends, it just begins anew. Each and every sound garden we all plant, each and every hand we reach out to assist the needy, each and every time we sing the praises of our own creator, we find health and love, and we accentuate the already accentuated heightened light of approval of the earthly beings. We are all in conjunction here; there is no plight for separation except the plight within. And as each person eliminates all the un-Godly aspects of themselves, it helps each of us to grow strong gallantly within so that our brothers and sisters may do the same.

Blessed be to all who read this, as it is a Pharaoh's welcome to you that we all state the following:

Blessed be the child in our arms that has fallen into a deep sleep; may he awaken and follow the pathway lit within so that he may follow his song in his soul. Simply be and simply live. This is the way of the Tao. And the Tao hath many more lifetimes to ring in, so become more aware of the plenty to whoever shall be put at your doorway or doorstep. The gladness and the tithing, so that the sad may arise. Not necessarily in terms of money or material giving's, but in terms of illuminating one's self so that the others may master themselves. As all are our own children of a holy blessed God within, and may all the shining blessings of the Holy Christed Being be within you this day. Amen.

Whoa now, that was heavy!

My dear, all challenges are simply self-made. I assure you, the times you have lost were really times you had won. The things you felt were very injurious to you were only openings for your soul to deepen your faith, and to open the deep wounds within, because, if none of this pain had happened in this lifetime, then none of these words would currently be written, and none of our brothers and sisters would be alerted to their power. The High Priestess once said, "In our worst hour in our life, we become hopeful in the drudgery of the soul, as out of the hasten past misuse of our will comes a bounty of reconstruction, and in this turmoil we find not haste, but solace within, and this is the real reason for any pain. All shall come from death to a vision for Christ and, in terms of light, we shall all become a vision for healing the universal shield of protection for the good. The long-term effects of the old veil or so-called protection have caused so many pain and destruction, yet, as the veil thins and lifts, all emotional ties to the past shall be gotten rid of, and all newness shall be granted. IN YOUR WOUND IS YOUR GOLD."

We ask of you who read this book to remedy your life with these actions and to become a living, breathing voice for man. Each man needs a wrench to fix his mismanaged life. Give up the old and live in the new, and the blessing of all that you felt passed you over will reside fully in your being from this day forward. All hail! What has been taken away shall return tenfold. It is in the letting go of the past that one re-lives, and awakens to the eternal light within. Blessings to all who come and read. They are the ones for whom the bell tolls.

King Arthur's Ring of Men Speak

Blessings from King Arthur's ring of men. We are all satisfactory here, and ready to assist. Blessed be the King, as well, as he has many a times been here for you all. Each time you feel the need for assistance, you may also call upon us for assistance, as we are the archbishops of the Holy Christed crown, and we are the holy backs upon which they stand in the hierarchy. Each coins the pharaoh, "Upon the backs of babes do we ride, only to live so deeply in disguise. For each man or woman sees only what they wish to see. Give unto your eyes, which only see the untruth, and allow them to literally stand open at attention."

All else will seemingly be ratified, for those who seek out the Holy Christed Being shall be the saviors of the Lord to come. Meaning that each person who arrives here at the light, or the light working station of these writings, shall begin to maintain a foraging of or for the Holy Christed Being—as in one way or another we all shall ascertain together as one. The quicker one stands tall upon our back of babes, the quicker world peace can be had and unite us as one for one in one for all, as a sort of revelry of one. It is as though the past has retreated from the future in order to live free once again. As we are being called in so many directions, we find it unnecessary for the marred to become unhinged as they are the Holy Christed one, yet they know it not. And in not knowing, they will at some point rise up. However if we each do our part and live this light of the Holy Christed Being within, they will notice our light. So each of us doing our part in holding our own Holy Christ light so bright as to be a beacon for humanity, and, in doing so, we align with the holy creator within to be the best that we can be, just for today. Then tomorrow we begin again. It is a simple, easy, 24-hour-a-day plan for living. Try it. You will never be disappointed. Carry on.

Thank you to King Arthur's court!

So the allegory here is: Be at peace with the holy gift inside, and proceed to give it away to thy brothers and thy sisters. In order to coincide together within, we must fully coincide without. There are no in-betweens—either we all live, or we all die. That is the point here. The more we give to our suffering soul brothers and sisters, the more we together shall rise.

There are no in-betweens any longer, and the longer we wait, the further they will be to reach

Well, we have foretold the story of Jesus being a leper. Let's reminisce about how lepers have a healing light within. They have been so turned away, they feel total shame, self-disgust, even suicidal. The shame-filled societal rejects are the ones harmed by the monsters of the societal hierarchical life here on earth. And the veils are very much lifted, so as to peek behind them. More will always be revealed. These are the real lepers. These are the real moneymakers who feel invincible. These are the patriarchal heads of state and church. These are the mind of a so-called different God. A God of man, greed and punishment to the good. Hierarchically, these people sit at the top, and the good stay at the bottom. It has seemingly always been that way, as the ones at the top have the ability to barter with money, or cash, or jewels, or man. In past times, they sold man for barter. Such a destructive act to one's soul. The forbidden legacy of hate that comes from that act. The slaves who were once men are now simply a piece of barter. The points in all of this today are:

1. Never allow your soul to be bartered.
2. Never sell your hallowed being for money.
3. Identify deeply with the fact that I am what I am, and no one can ever buy the bounty of my soul.

These are the God-given rules to be lived with intense love and humility.

The ones who try to make you pay with your soul are not men of God, they are men of money. Yes, they have the ability to become men of God, but absolutely no power to acknowledge this. They only see dollar signs, and that is their mission. This is the lethargy of the earth. The fallen have left so that their brethren may have a chance to heal.

Master Jesus explains reincarnation

What does this mean?

It means that some of the souls who leave earth prematurely are trying to give their brethren a chance to see the signals. That as one's soul dies, and releases the humanity in his or her body, the peacekeepers take that body and heal it.

The rest of the souls are magnified here on earth until another time, to come back if they wish.

Do most of them wish to come back, or only very few?

Mostly those with unfinished business here, where they think that they can make some sort of difference.

These are the real enlightened beings?

Like yourself, your mother, your children. You all have had many lives here, trying to change the meaning of life by assisting in their healing for so many. And you all keep trying and maybe, finally, this is the break you have all been seeking.

Let's hope so.

Now. Turnabout is fair play. Let me ask: What is the final chapter of this book going to be about?

Well, my friend, it is going to be about you. Your life. And how you explicitly became God.

Really? Why would anyone be interested in that?

Well, have you not achieved this goal?

Well, yes, I have.

Then carry on and write.

I feel like this would be the most boring part of this book.

On the contrary! It will be the most interesting, the most confident, and the most heroic thing you have ever done in your life. You are going to share your life with others so that they may live better. Go on, and begin.

Mantra for the day:

Thought for the day:

Today I am in deep awareness of the good in myself that I have found to be God. May I live this way forever.

Chapter 23
Day 21 – The Final Chapter: About Me

As I sit here to write this, I am really doing my best to find other things to do. I really do not like writing about myself or, (let's be honest) my human self. So it is apparent I will write about the God self. The light inside, or, the illuminated vibration that I have found to be true.

As I have had many life trials and tribulations, this light inside has never failed me. Even almost to the point of suicide. Yes I have to write about it, I contemplated suicide at one point when my life fell apart. I felt so absolutely hopeless. At this point, something stopped me, I always like to think it was the love of my children, but I am now being told, as I write once again with tears welling up in my eyes, it was my own speculation I had not known about the inside. It was I, it was you, it was God—and it was terrifying!

As I sit here, I remember that final moment I have written about in the previous chapters, when I cried out to God, or whatever I thought it was at the time. I cried out to an entity I had heard about, or an icon I had seen on my grandmothers' walls, to a "something" other than myself. This is a good characterization of what it was to me at that time. A non-entity, a non-judicial being, who was both the judge and jury of my hope. I revealed this capacity to state in so many words during a time of total and complete desperation for change. Please, God, help me!

And boom—it happened!

I knew the next right thing to do. I called a rehab center and was there the next day. That quickly, that fast, and that irreverently. I was so disenfranchised from who I was inside that I found peace in an honest, desperate call for help to something, somewhere, somehow. I cried.

And then it all began.

My Sobriety in a Nutshell
Year 1

This is what I was facing, or what I had created prior to knowing that I am God.

Bad stuff:
- I was an alcoholic.
- I was prosecuting my husband for domestic violence.
- I was going through a divorce.

- I kept going back and forth between two men, even though I had a restraining order against the man I was divorcing.
- I lived at my parents' house, where my dad was drinking way too much.
- I kept putting my children back and forth through all of this.

Good stuff:
- I wasn't drinking a day at a time.
- I found a place of belonging where there were people like me who had similar issues with their drinking
- I found God through Alcoholics Anonymous and by working their 12 Steps.
- I successfully prosecuted my ex-husband for domestic violence, and that was the last time anyone ever hit me, or that I hit anyone else.
- I got divorced.
- I learned to become a better mother, and not to scream at my children.
- I found a good job.
- I found an apartment.*
- 9-months sober, I was catapulted into a relationship with God such as I had never imagined.

*see note on this apartment

At work one day, I overheard two women talking about domestic violence. My ears perked up. They said victims of domestic violence can get help from a statewide program funded by abusers, who are prosecuted and ordered to pay restitution for their crimes. I peaked my head into their cubicle and asked for the program's telephone number. I signed up, I got out of my parents' house, where my dad was drinking and my mom was a bit crazy and I moved into a safe place for me any my children. The California Victims Witness Program funded my moving, and my first step to personal freedom. And it gave me time to begin writing and having conversations with God.

It also allowed me to create a safe and loving environment for my children.

Year 2

I went to paralegal school, while also working full-time, going to AA meetings, and rearing my children 70% of the time. I was able to achieve this with assistance from my family and friends.

Year 3

I received an AA Degree in Paralegal Studies.

Working the 12-Step program of Adult Children of Alcoholics enabled me to see how I had been affected by my own and by other people's behavior, and I began healing those two parts of myself: 1) The broken part, which I was drinking to compensate for my own personal brokenness, and 2) The part of me that was broken by other people's abusive behavior.

After working the Alanon 12-Steps, I felt truly whole as a human being, and I felt the God-light within me continuing to grow. I read *You Can Heal Your Life*, by Louise Hay, and realized I could change the way I saw and thought about myself. I felt I had hit the lottery, as I began to have a different conversation with my soul.

I realized that all the contrary things people had said to me had been wrong. Negative thoughts, especially about myself, that I grew up believing, were all wrong. I got a chance to change them. I began to live my life with purity of thought, mind, body, and soul. These efforts were re-doubled. I was still in a crazy relationship with a married man. He was getting a divorce, and we were planning to get married, but I realized two things: 1) Any relationship that begins in untruth will never work, and 2) No matter how good someone looks, or seems to look on paper, or how otherwise perfect they appear, if they create inner chaos for you, they cannot truly be right for you.

Accordingly, I ended this relationship, but without assigning any blame or judgment. Rather, it was because I needed to seek my OWN truth, for once, and not just accept what other people might think is good for me. This was the first time I heard God speak to me, and I acted upon these words by ending the relationship, even knowing there would be backlash from my work, my friends, and my family, because in my gut I knew that it was the right thing to do for myself.

Hearing God's Voice

I began a relationship with a man at the end of my drinking. This man was perfect in all aspects of finding a mate. However, something kept feeling "off" for me. On paper he was magnificent, and as a human he had all the right traits one would seek to be a husband and father to my children. However, I kept feeling spun in my head and in my gut, and I could not figure out why this was not perfect. I went running one morning and, as I was about to finish my run, I heard a voice say, "He's got to go." And I said back, "OK. If I do this, then you will know that I trust You." That was it—the beginning of being clear enough by working on myself and doing all these lessons in this book, I heard God. That was the very first time I heard God speak to me, and I listened and then I took action.

Ending the relationship caused us both deep sadness, but I knew it was the right thing for ME.

I stayed single for some time—going through so many emotions and asking God why no one loved me. All this after I broke up with the best man I felt I could ever find, or that I even thought I deserved at the time. Then, after a dark night of the romantic soul, things began to change.

Year 4

During this time I did an exercise called "Build a Man" with my AA sponsor. I listed all the things I wanted in a partner, what things were acceptable to me, and what I truly wanted in a mate. Then I prayed. I began to get promotions at work, and was really on my A game in life. I was promoted to legal assistant at a different agency. My life looked good, on my own, without a man.

What I didn't know was that I had worked for over 10 years in a building with toxic mold. I began to suffer depression, listlessness, nose bleeds, weight loss, and a kind of virtual dementia—confusion and forgetting how to do even simple tasks at work. I saw several doctors about these symptoms, to no avail. My symptoms had not emerged until after I left that toxic building. Other workers in that building experienced severe illness including internal hemorrhage, cancers, and some even died. For the following few years, I believed this illness had caused my personal downfall.

In April I began dating my current husband who was also at the beginning of a new life. When he ultimately moved in with us, he had one suitcase. But he was the most gentle, loving, kind, caring, and considerate man I had ever met. (Also, he met all the criteria on my "List"!)

As he began to succeed in his work, I began to fail. I lost my good job because I was unable to perform as before. I had sharp, stabbing pains in my shoulders. But doctors could find nothing wrong. There was no explanation for my illness, and therefore there was "nothing they could do." I was finished.

I felt the hand of God heavy on me at the time. I had to utter the hardest words of my life to a man: "I need your help!" Then he began to help me financially, but I bounced from job to job over the next few years, trying to find my way.

Years 5-19

In my 12th year of sobriety, I went to see a Reiki healer, because I could not breathe. I could not work, I could barely take care of my children and, the worst thing of all, the doctors could find nothing wrong with me. After about 8 trips to the doctor, the last doctor said, you have a spiritual dis-ease. Do you understand, and I said yes. He told me he was a Reiki Master from Australia, and suggested I go see a Reiki Healer. So, I went, I got healed, and I began taking Reiki classes. In the first class, I began seeing moving pictures in my left eye. I began knowing things, feeling things, and healing others. Reiki, I believe, reawakened something in me that I had already had at one point in a past life. After my grandmother died that same year, I began to hear, and see, and listen to a spirit. At first I did not know what to do, but my left knee would hurt deeply each time a spirit wanted to communicate, and that was my indicator—my knee. A funny thing about this pain is, when my grandmother was dying, right before she passed, I felt a pain in my left knee like I had never felt before, and then she died. I believe she passed her gift to me on her death bed. And that is how I began seeing fully.

During these years of my sobriety, I worked at least 50 jobs in the legal and executive field. At each new job, I found someone who needed healing—be it cancer, alcohol, drugs, divorce, death, you name it. It was almost as though they had prayed for help from God, and I showed up. This went on for several years. Finally, I took a position working for a woman whose mother had just died. In this job, I was paid the most I had ever made, and it was with a very prestigious law firm. The woman was the most narcissistic woman I had ever met—self-absorbed, defiant, dishonest, and headstrong, she never once asked me about myself or about my private life. Therefore, I believe, missing the hand of God. I made more mistakes working for her than I had ever made before. I looked so inept and disorganized. After only 6 months, I left and never looked back. That was the last time I worked as a paralegal. I believe it had to be so horrific that I would stop looking for that to be my job in society. Almost like, I needed to be broken of it.

During this time, my husband rose from that one suitcase to working for and building a thriving business. He told me it was OK for me to stop working, and that he would support me in my spiritual work. He is a literal Godsend! I have never felt unsafe or in harm's way with him. God fashioned our lives together in a way that has enabled me to do my work from a home, filled with love, dignity, respect, and God. This allows me to do soul healing and clearing, to learn and teach Reiki, and to work directly with the spiritual realm, listening, channeling, and divinely inspiring others. All because I cried out for help to a God I did not then understand.

So this last chapter is about surrender. Not in the sense of giving up something, but rather as the way of beginning something out of nothing.

The real fight is over, and the simple surrender suffices. All is found in the laying down of our swords to render our soul enlightened.

Sir Walter Raleigh speaks:
Good morning, Sir Walter!
Good morning, old friend!
How are you this bright morning?
Substantially blown away by your coming in.
Why?
I don't know; you have never really come into my mind before.
I am here. I stand by until needed, just like we all do. Preferably when one is in dire need of an admission of one's faith, and you are starting to stonewall your wits by using common sense about them, so here I am to assist you.
Thank you, Sir Walter!

Bring back the jolly old self from the reunion of the Holy Christed Being, in other words. Keep thy plot on the dire need for service to our souls.

Here you lay down your plentiful experience. Now lay down your plentiful knowledge of who you are at the core of your being. The absolute memento of the Holy Christed child being born and bred into existence by your own tyranny, of sorts. Begin slowly by marking your existence to the past, but now fully blow these readers out of the proverbial water with your casting of grace.

Allow for the mere sight of your soul to be weathered hope for those who have none at the moment. There is a fallacy about God, or Christ, or man, or the heavens—that they, or it, are primarily a farce, and in the Lord's so-called God-given book, man is the simple argument for Christ. When in truth, you are, or Christ is, or the manner of Christ through to the homegrown vibration of a mortal man has nothing to do with Christ. Christ is at all talk of the abode, if you ask me. The past humans gave to him a name, only for it to become a sheer farce. And we are seeing it more and more clearly through the saying son of God, or God of man.

So you, my dearest friend here on earth, reunify one's soul to the place of their beginning. Take them each back to that space of light, of sound, of song. Here is your duty to life, to Christ, and to the past people who have been put in harm's way because of their so-called God or Christ. Through, or under the guise of, the church. Give these people back their soul life—once and for all.

Well, Sir Walter, I hope I am doing that here. I will be writing another book for those souls who have been harmed. But I need to finish this one first.

The Catholic church has gone bonkers on, and hit the ceiling with, the faith of their so-called God and their yearning for gold and souls of man, boys, children, etc. Each and every brother they touched, and humiliated, and hurt, and destroyed was a God-given human soul, and they took each one without manner of their own soul for hire.

They were given a so-called gift from God, in a manner to be used for good, and mastered it in terms of, "Behold, I am Godly, I wear gold, hear me, I am right!"

All of this is horse hound, and definitely against anything that God would have anyone do. Please sit.
Ok.
Now, each savage who has hurt another has a right to God, yes?
Yes.
And each savage who began as a soul, as one of our many, has become decrepit with greed, yes?
Yes.
And these souls, which are many, can and will arbitrarily reunify their own Holy Christed Being inside and go to the other side blindsided, not even knowing who they are or what they provide here.

They will ultimately go to the grail of the pail of pain and hurt for many, and become reunified through the pain of the hurt.

When one is hurt here, they will reunify on the other side. It is a give-and-take. So in saying this, you find it a bit disturbing, yes?
Yes. As I feel that God's children should be saved.
True, but even a few can be saved by eliminating others' pain. So, as they go there in death and become sort of reunified, they will be sent somewhere other

than earth to re-sanctify their souls. No time is ever wasted again on these dire ones; they are driven from the universal sanctity of good and are brought or taken back to the place of their own remittance.

The heaven of a so-called hell, if you will, and they will begin to articulate their own heaven within at some point, maybe.

Well, shall I even put this in the book?

Sure. Why not? Hell is a nature of man, not God. Man creates his own hell by his own actions, and being. As one being, we cannot be responsible for all beings. Everyone has their own natural ability to think, so they must use it. And this, my friend, is called service.

Your service to earth and to the Godly realm is to convince the Christ inside others to formally reintroduce itself to them, or to their soul. By simply stating the following prayer with Martin Luther as sincerely as they can muster:

Prayer with Martin Luther

All beings of God and creation—On this day, I solemnly and ultimately give back to me, my own honor, my own service, my own life, to something that is so deep within me, I didn't even know it was hidden. How in fact may I release my duty to cause?

I open my heart and solemnly give my own self the freedom to fathom my own talents, my own freedom, my own light within to be open, honest, and latently undiversified in the quagmire of my life. I am now as honest, as open, and as willing as the dying may be.

I give now my will and my own life over to the Holy Christed Being within; this is only a vibration, a spiritual chalice of God. A long-standing resonance of the Holy Christed Being that has come from creation to me. This once-holy vibration resumed its presence in me on the day I was born.

And since that very day, I have held this sacred song within my being and on this day, I am relinquishing the determination of how to manage it over to that same creation vibration I begin with:

I lead by example each day by knowing the vibration of creation of our creator God within. And I know that this holy vibration is one of mass, electrons, showmanship in terms of being within, by being and giving from that delicate space from within. This is now my duty to Christ, my duty to my own creation, and my duty to life. I heal myself deeply within this holy crevice of Christ, for it is here that I reside. I give this residence the name of _____ so that I have no ignorance of imbalance or defamation to it.

I wish for no turmoil to come from naming it a different being, as I distrust the old naming of the source. I have a freedom to be within this holy crevice named _____ at all times.

I awaken with it
I imagine with it
I create with it
I live with it.
As this is me,

This is my name,
And this is my child.
I am me.
Blessed be.
All will finally be well.
All is forgiven and just.
Amen.

This is a gift to you from the Holy Christed child within. Blessed be thy name. Live forevermore with continued gratitude, and longing for the great vibration to continue to exist, for it is in this vibration that we all create heaven on earth. Let us be the first generation to make a change in the unilateral resonance to create a universal resonance. If we all be ourselves at our core, we will all be God to the universe. Then we will all be brothers and sisters of the greatest vibration of light and love.

All hail the queen!

Blessings to all for whom the bell tolls.

Amen.

Mantra for the day:

Thought for the day:

Today I give my gift of vibration to all. May I live this way forevermore.

Conclusion

As I sit and finish this final chapter, having read all of these words from all who have chosen to come and assist, I am in deep appreciation to you, the reader, and to all who persisted in encouraging my writing this book. There is so much need for this work, that it can no longer be hidden in the atrocity of man. It boggles my mind why no one has stated such thoughts before. I wish for this to be read loudly, and proudly, and in the highest pitch of vibration. I can only hope for a grand illusion to be busted open and the purest of truths be lived here on earth for our children, our grandchildren and our ancestors. They deserve solace. All who have died in the name of God, for the cause of God and for God explicitly, I write this:

We are all in need of a comingled forgiveness barter. I forgive you, you forgive me, and we live free together in Christ.

Our lives are made up of so much constructed turmoil, yet no one even sees it. So this book is written to lift the veil of forgetfulness and to reopen one's eyes to the truth of the old statement of I am God, I live God, God resides in me, and I in Him.

The purest of surrender is needed to start a new life. Give it up, give it over, and get going. You have a purpose—find it, live it, be it. That is the only simple term of being a human. Let's all pray on this idea and close, so that the next unimaginable book can be written.

I thank each and every one of you for reading this book. Blessed be, in so many forms. All is well.

On this final day, I ask for all guides, masters, ascended masters and our higher selves to be present. We ascertain on this final 21st day of this writing, that I, Andrea Elizabeth, hereby allow for all my brethren to reside deeply within my heart and soul to become full-fledged, promised souls of light. As we sit here in the openness as God beside the masters and in the wellness and beauty of this day, we are ascending the veil to enlightenment through so many avenues not stated before. We are here through hope, grace, and antiquity. Each and every enlightened being present gives of their hope and blessings, and their magnificence of light. Sit in this glory and be fully present. This is the gift we are allowed as humans.

Each day sit in the full presence of the light and breathe it all in. This is a perfect way to begin a new day by releasing the old to allow in the new. Blessings to each and every one of you.

All is perfection on this day.

So be it!

Andrea's websites:
www.spiritualenergyhealingguide.com
https://www.beurownreligion.com/

Facebook: https://www.facebook.com/andreaelizabeth2020/

YouTube: https://www.youtube.com/channel/UCCX0V_sGJTh9wDZlA0WLPyA/featured?view_as=public

Patreon: https://www.patreon.com/AndreaElizabeth

www.ingramcontent.com/pod-product-compliance
Lightning Source LLC
Chambersburg PA
CBHW071448080526
44587CB00014B/2035